Coin Collecting Bible

The #1 Beginner to Advanced Coin Book

Learn the Replicable Strategies to Start Your Coin Collection, Uncover Hidden Treasure, and Avoid Worst Counterfeits or Scam

by

Rob Quarterman

Table of Contents

✿ HERE IS YOUR FREE GIFT!

Gain exclusive access to the world of coins with special free bonuses! Get your hands on our free **Coin Identification Guide** and enjoy FREE ACCESS to **Coin Hub** to understand how to take coin collecting to the next level. This essential pack is your golden ticket to achieving your coin-collecting objectives and avoiding collector risks, all through clear and replicable strategies. Unlock these free resources by scanning the QR code below.

Start your simplified journey to success in the coin-collecting field today! Scan now and collect confidently, free from misinformation, the risk of overpaying, the pitfalls of grading, and the ever-present threat of online scams!

SCAN THE QR CODE TO DOWNLOAD THE COIN IDENTIFICATION GUIDE AND ENJOY FREE ACCESS TO THE COIN HUB.

OR CLICK THE LINK https://qrco.de/ber52u

How Can You Help with This book?

Writing this book turned out to be quite the challenge, indeed, debugging now seems like a walk in the park compared to the writing process. I've hit writer's block for the first time in my life. Understanding the topics is one thing, but trying to lay them out logically, concisely, cohesive, and well-organized is a whole different ball game.

Also, since I decided to steer clear of any publishing houses, I can proudly call myself an "independent author." It's a personal choice that hasn't been without its struggles, but my dedication to helping others has won out.

That's why I'd be incredibly grateful if you could provide some feedback on Amazon. Your input would mean a lot to me and would greatly help me share this material with others. Here's what I recommend:

1. **If you haven't already, scan the QR code** at the start of the book download the Coin Identification Guide and enjoy FREE ACCESS to Coin Hub.

2. **Scan the QR code below or simply click the link and leave quick feedback on Amazon!**

CLICK THE LINK https://qrco.de/ber72N

The best approach? Share a short video sharing your thoughts on the book! If that seems too much, no pressure at all. Feedback along with a couple of photos of the book would still be greatly appreciated!

Note: There's no obligation, but it would be immensely appreciated!

I'm excited to embark on this journey with you. Ready to dive in?
Happy reading!

Introduction
Why You Should Collect Coins
Today

Introduction to Numismatics and Coin Collecting

Collecting coins is no different from collecting certain types of works of art, first-edition books, or antique stamps. The truth is that everyone has a different reason for collecting coins.

The initial idea of why collecting comes from the human desire to accumulate items related to the same species, following a process of observation and search.

Collecting can be considered a passion, and like all passions, it allows us to move to another world. Passion is something inexplicable, it is something magical, and magical is precisely one of our names for the inexplicable (Herzinger). It involves studying, classifying, seeing, reviewing, and manipulating. It creates an emotional relationship with collectibles but also uneasiness, a frustration when they are not available (Arminana).

Numismatics focuses on everything related to coins, everything that has had the function of money, and everything related to it. Thus we mainly find coins, medals, and banknotes. There are also casino chips and jetons, which usually rub shoulders with other related objects such as decorations and sigillography, for example.

As is well known, it is from 1960 when numismatic-related activities like clubs, auctions, conventions, meetings, flea markets, fairs, and meetings began to be born. The expansion of coin collecting has been mainly due to two causes: on the one hand, there is the desire to own objects with historical and artistic value, and on the other hand, the need to find a haven where to invest all or part of the savings.

Who Collects Coins Today?

Nowadays, more and more people or collectors are approaching numismatics. This science is considered a hobby that fills many with satisfaction and facilitates intellectual growth by acquiring new knowledge.

When speaking directly of people who collect objects of this type, we must refer to people who perform an activity for physical pleasure, and it seems that the search for and acquisition of new items for a collection generates dopamine, the neurotransmitter responsible for states of joy, well-being, and pleasure.

Precisely, it is from a set of human profiles linked to the act of collecting that determines the collector's figure.

Another collector profile refers to the person who gathers objects to have knowledge and to know the root of things, and an example are numismatic collections, philatelic collections, antique book collections, etc.

Certainly, what this book reveals is that whoever collects treasures is not for the object itself but for what it can provide information with which to interpret reality.

A Fast-Growing Hobby with Which You Can Earn Money

The truth is that in addition to producing pleasure, this hobby is currently of great interest because it is positioned as one of those that generate income.

Coin collecting has become one of those markets where rare or unique pieces are presented as exclusive objects for which people give more money every day. Certainly, they do this to satisfy their desires and pleasures.

Subsequently, once the piece is acquired, others choose to wait for a while, and after satisfying their desires to acquire a unique piece, they decide to sell them since it is an excellent and lucrative option.

Why Should You Collect Coins Today?

Here are some reasons you should know if you are thinking about collecting coins:

1. *Coins as a new way to diversify your investment portfolio*

If you are thinking of investing in something and you like collecting, you should know that this activity is a way to obtain valuable assets. You can start collecting from free coins to more special coins that require an investment. The important point is that to do so you must know and learn to identify the type of piece and what makes it special among many others. You will learn more about this later!

2. *A hobby not only for the rich*

Commonly, collecting is usually related to people with purchasing power since it is known that investments in rare or unique coins can be substantial. However, this is not the definitive context because numismatics is also related to knowing and finding historical facts related to wars, empires, monarchs, the evolution of art, architecture, traditions of nations, etc., through these pieces. It is presented as a way to unite the past and the present.

3. *Earn money with your passion and skills instead of relying on investment banking*

When it comes to making money on your own, many people think of investing in a business that can bring you good money in the long term and in a sustainable way. However, in the case of coin collecting, what you need to do is to make a first investment and perhaps sporadically others; the truth is that just by acquiring a couple of coins, you can start your business without relying so much on investments. You will be able to determine that from the following chapters.

4. *The dream of finding a hidden treasure: find out if your coin collection locked in a drawer for years or perhaps inherited from a family member has some kind of value and can be auctioned*

In some cases, people often have an inheritance or simply keep very valuable objects without knowing it. That is why it is necessary to know much more information about this type of piece.

As previously mentioned, numismatics is not only a hobby for people with purchasing power but also for people with knowledge. In these cases, it is necessary to be more rigorous with the information and especially the history of the items you keep because you may have a great treasure there.

5. *Involve your children in an activity that will bring them closer and make them more passionate about each other and that they will leave as their legacy*

There is nothing more enjoyable than sharing a hobby with a child, and what better than a coin collection to do so? Without knowing it, a coin collection can represent a fortune in the future for your family.

6. *It is the first choice for investment*

Since the 19th century, the interest in the academic knowledge of coins has progressively increased until it has become a branch of historical divulgation.

It is in this way that the methodology has spread internationally and collaborates in situating and knowing the different aspects of history. The collection of coins, rather than being a hobby, is nowadays presented as a way to gain knowledge, a channel to describe histories.

It can simply be said that this activity provides valuable knowledge of historical periods and the role played by the monetary and economic spheres of each society.

Regardless of the reason you are interested in coin collecting, below you will find a comprehensive and **practical 5-step method** that can help collectors like you achieve their goals.

Thank you very much for your curiosity to discover my 5-step method for making your coin-collecting investment profitable and avoiding mistakes. Inside, you'll discover the best strategies that I chose to help you achieve your coin-collecting objectives and prevent the following risks for collectors:

- *As you'll know, making money in this competitive marketplace requires recognizing opportunities.*

For this reason, the **first and second steps of the method** will allow you to quickly understand the sectoral trends in the coin market and the best strategies for learning the system that makes this market profitable.

- *If you buy rare coins on the Internet, you're most likely to get ripped off by sellers without vital caveats on bidding in online auctions.*
That's why the **third step of the method** will permit you to source and select valuable coins that fit your collecting goals and provide you with the top tips for finding hidden gems for your collection.

- *In addition, grading-related abuses persist in less obvious forms, and these remain the most significant source of potential losses for consumers/investors.*
And this is the reason why the **fourth and fifth steps of the method** were thought to avoid counterfeits and proper coin care. You will learn to spot counterfeit coins and avoid scams while discovering how to properly store, display, and care for your coin collection to preserve its value.

- *Finally, as you know, many thousands of dollars can be lost, too, if you let Uncle Sam pick your pocket with zero up-to-date and expanded tax-slashing strategies.*
Therefore, you'll receive exclusive access to the *Coin Collecting HUB*, which provides insider tips and tricks from seasoned collectors.

The book includes two valuable bonuses:

1) **BONUS 1**: The *Coin Identification Guide*, which includes a selection of the most interesting coins updated to 2025, provides you with current market values and insights, with a specific focus on American, British, Canadian, and Australian coins. The ebook contains images of the coins described in the book.

2) **BONUS 2**: Free access to the *Coin Collecting HUB*, which represents your personal treasure map of the rarest coins and includes a series of videos on how to take your coin collection to the next level.

Thanks again, and happy reading.

STEP I:

UNLOCK THE HIDDEN WORLD OF COIN COLLECTING: DISCOVER WHY THIS HOBBY IS A GOLDMINE!

Chapter 1:
The Collectible Coin Market

Coins are certainly an easy-to-invest asset that can grow your investment over time and bring you pleasure. Many luxury pieces are constantly on the market for sale to collectors, but few people know the value that these pieces can represent. That is why you will learn about the coin market in this chapter.

What Are the Sectorial Trends in the Coin Market?

Collectible coins can be part of a large investment portfolio. Although if you start your collection with the idea of investing, you should keep in mind that the value of collectibles does not always respond to market trends and that valuations respond to other factors.

In the case of numismatic collections, the objective is to obtain rare coins. Remember that the rarer they are, the more valuable they will be. Although, as a business, they can generate good profits, keep in mind that getting them takes some time, and this is where you should focus.

Therefore, investing in antique or collectible coins is profitable if you understand what you are doing, and the best thing is that you will be fulfilling your desires at the same time. Although they can be considered good investments, collectible coins do not figure as substitutes for instruments such as bonds and debt securities that can help you achieve your short- and medium-term goals. However, collectible coins do add some diversification to your investment portfolio.

Another detail that collectors should consider is that the coin market has become less risky thanks to the existence of identification and verification services. Now the Internet also helps, as it allows you to learn much more about numismatics and collecting.

It can be said that when it comes to coins, as with stamp collecting, these are presented as tangible collectibles, but not all of them are useful or can be used for investment.

Many aspects contribute to the price of the most valuable coins. The main ones are typically rarity, demand, and quality. The value of rare U.S. and foreign coins can also be affected by external market factors, such as inflation, the performance of other investment vehicles, and government policies.

1. *Coins as an investment: traditional and alternative haven asset*

Paper investments represent partial ownership of a company, and the value of those assets will rise and fall with the company's value. While paper or digital stocks have no intrinsic value in and of themselves, coins, because they are made of precious metals such as gold and silver, do have intrinsic value and may also have collectible value.

While the value of investment coins lies primarily in their precious metal content, the value of rare coins is determined primarily by their quality, rarity, and historical significance, which is the extrinsic value of the coin. In addition, each investor has full control over the type and quantity of coins in his or her portfolio, but the vast majority of equity investors have little control over the shares of the company in which they invest.

For collectors in the *UK*, coins from the reigns of King George III and Queen Victoria are particularly valued for their historical significance. *Australian* collectors should look for pre-decimal coins, such as those from the early 20th century.

2. *Collecting coins is more fashionable than collecting bullion and is also less risky*

It can be said that it is a fashion because more and more people are getting involved in this hobby. If collecting is an exercise of observation and search, among many other points, we can define numismatics as the hobby or art of collecting coins from any period or country.

Numismatics is also defined as the science that deals with the knowledge of coins and medals, mainly ancient ones. A definition closer to the world of collecting would present numismatics as the hobby or art of collecting coins of any period or country.

Joining local numismatic societies in your country can provide networking opportunities and access to exclusive coin shows and auctions. In the *US*, consider joining the American Numismatic Association (ANA). In *Canada*, the Royal Canadian Numismatic Association (RCNA) is a valuable resource.

Why Invest in Numismatic Coins and Numismatic Coin Collectibles?

In recent years, more and more people have decided to invest in certain types of historical coins to preserve their heritage. Many economic media and industry professionals believe that a recession is more than likely looming in many Western economies, with volatile currencies and rising inflation.

This situation does not offer investors many guarantees. As a result, many savers find it challenging to preserve their capital. Those who choose the classic options, such as bank accounts, deposits, or mutual funds, barely make a return.

Many savers and investors are diversifying their strategy and have found in the numismatic market a haven. When talking about benefits, the certainty is that there are many because the greatest virtue of numismatics is that, unlike certain financial assets, the coin is a tangible good, increasingly in demand, scarce, and durable.

Another great advantage, and the one mentioned above, is that this asset offers a high return over the years. Some collectors value the almost immediate liquidity they can obtain, thanks to the fact that it is possible to sell the pieces anywhere in the world. In addition, numismatics can better withstand macroeconomic swings and currency risk.

During economic downturns, focus on acquiring coins with high intrinsic metal value, such as *gold sovereigns* from the *UK* or *American Gold Eagles*. These coins tend to retain value better during inflationary periods.

There is a popular belief that any coin has a high capacity for revaluation, and there is an erroneous tendency to think that any relatively recent coin of any material can be sold for exorbitant prices after a few years. It is necessary to receive expert advice.

This is precisely the service that a recognized numismatic auction house should offer to its clients, making sure that the pieces selected meet certain conditions, depending on their state of conservation, provenance, material (in most cases, they are gold or silver pieces), place of minting, scarcity and revaluation potential.

The difference between the starting and selling prices of some old coins recently sold at auctions attests to their demand in the collector's market.

The Advantages of Investing in Coins

Tax advantages: there are several tax advantages to owning rare coins. These include possible sales tax exemptions and the fact that growth in the value of rare coins is not taxed until they are sold. This is different from obtaining annual tax returns from banks and stock accounts.

Of course, the benefits of investing in both bullion and numismatic coins extend beyond taxes.

The Performance of Rare Coin Investments Over the Past Three Decades

High-end (origin/quality) coins have outperformed inventories, and investors are encouraged to choose quality rare coins. Quality rare coins outperformed all other asset classes in the first three years of the study.

Another advantage of investing in rare coins is that novice collectors and investors on a limited budget can find good quality coins with upside potential in a variety of price ranges. Understanding how to buy quality investment coins and how to leverage their value is your best guarantee of profit and security.

For beginners, starting with widely recognized and easily verifiable coins, such as *Morgan Silver Dollars* from the *US or Canadian Maple Leafs*, can be a safe way to enter the market.

Unlock the Secret to Growing Wealth: Why Collectible Coins Are the New Investment Frontier!

Here are several reasons to diversify your portfolio with an investment asset that can be considered a leisure asset and a serious investment:

1. *Collectible Coins as Accessible Investments*

When it comes to collecting without investing, you can start with simple and common coins like the ones that pass through your hands. So, you can take your first steps in the art of numismatics, satisfy your needs for pleasure and be closer to history.

2. *Collectible Coins as Affordable Investment*

Although coins can be part of an investment portfolio, you should keep an eye on some keys before doing so, but above all, you should do it affordably. You can do this little by little.

Tip: Look for beginner-friendly coin series like the *UK's Royal Mint Beatrix Potter* series or *Australia's Lunar series*, which are both affordable and have the potential for future appreciation

3. *Collectible Coins as Tangible and Practical investments*

If you wish to elevate your collecting to a more serious level, where the investment is substantial and requires knowledge, focus on unique pieces with specific details and special features. Understanding the field thoroughly is essential because these investments are often in rare and high-demand coins.

Tip: Consider focusing on coins like *Canadian Maple Leafs* or *Australian Kangaroos* for their recognized value and liquidity in the market.

4. *Coins vs. Cryptocurrencies: Tangibility and Historical Value*

Cryptocurrency, also called virtual currency, only exists electronically and is highly speculative. In contrast, collectible or investment coins are tangible assets with historical significance. They represent a piece of history and have intrinsic value due to their metal content and extrinsic value due to their historical context. Understanding the historical context of coins, such as *Australian pre-decimal coins* or significant *British commemorative coins*, can greatly enhance their value and your appreciation as a collector.

Chapter 2:

Investment Coins and Numismatic Collectible Coins

In this chapter, you will discover which coins are collectibles and which investment coins are worth targeting. While both are in demand for their value, it is important to know what distinguishes them.

This is a concept that is present in collecting circles, frequently being the compilation of both ancient coins and coins of various origins, that is, from multiple geographic places.

What Categories of Coins Are the Most Demanded by Coin Collectors?

Coins of precious materials: The most valuable *American coins* are gold eagles with unique characteristics and rare and valuable silver dollars such as the Dollar Bust Draped 1804 "Walter H. Childs." Some highly sought-after nickels by collectors, such as the Liberty Head Nickel 1913 "Louis E. Eliasberg," and some very valuable pennies, such as the Flowing Hair Cents.

For *UK collectors*, gold sovereigns from the Victorian era are highly prized.

Canadian collectors should consider the "Voyageur" dollar coins, especially those minted in 1935.

Rare coins: These happen to be the most sought-after coins by coin collectors. It is these pieces that are listed as rare or scarce with a high degree of preservation.

Australian collectors might find pre-decimal coins, such as the 1930 penny, highly valuable.

Silver Dollars, Cents, or Nickels: Certain coins have very high prices and characteristics that make them highly valued by buyers.

Look for coins with historical significance, such as those minted during significant historical events or reigns.

Coins That Have a Market

Currently, in the market, several coins are in demand, and the most recognized are:

American Eagle of the United States

It is a 22-karat gold investment coin minted by the United States Mint in 1986 after being approved by the US Congress. The obverse shows the Statue of Liberty wrapped in an American flag.

For its 35th anniversary, its reverse was modified. Thus, the male flying eagle approaching the nest has been replaced by the head of this bird.

American Buffalo, of the United States

Another of the most popular U.S. Mint investment coins, it was issued in June 2006 and is 999.9 thousandths (24 karats) of pure gold. The obverse features a portrait of a Native American, and the word "freedom" is written on it.

The year of mintage also appears in homage to the first inhabitants of that country. The reverse shows a buffalo on top of a mound "as a symbol of the pioneer spirit of the westward expansion of the American nation."

British Sovereign of the United Kingdom

The British Sovereign is one of the most famous gold coins in the world. Minted in 1817, it has a gold purity of 22 carats (91.67%). The obverse features the reigning monarch, while the reverse traditionally shows St. George slaying the dragon. The Sovereign is highly regarded for its historical significance and stability as an investment.

Collectors should look for Victorian-era sovereigns, especially those from the early reign of Queen Victoria, as they are particularly valued.

Canadian Maple Leaf of Canada

The Canadian Maple Leaf is a 24-karat gold coin minted by the Royal Canadian Mint in 1979. It is renowned for its high purity and beautiful design, featuring the image of Queen Elizabeth II on the obverse and a maple leaf on the reverse. The Maple Leaf is one of the most popular and widely traded bullion coins globally.

Special editions, such as the 1998 10th-anniversary coin, are highly sought after by collectors.

Australian Kangaroo of Australia

The Australian Kangaroo, also known as the Gold Nugget, is a 24-karat gold coin first issued by the Perth Mint in 1986. The design features a kangaroo, which changes annually, making it a favourite among collectors. The obverse depicts Queen Elizabeth II. The coin is celebrated for its high purity and artistic design.

Early editions from the 1980s and 1990s, particularly those with limited mintage, are highly valued.

Numismatic Collectible Coins vs Investment Coins

Unlike collectible coins, investment coins like the Krugerrand, Kangaroo, or American Eagles never circulate like the old coins.

What makes them so special is that gold and silver were used for their creation in a very primitive minting press compared to today. The coins were then placed in burlap bags and moved across the country by train, ship, and other means of transportation.

When these coins reached the banks, they had several bag marks from rubbing against each other along the way. So, there were certainly no coins that graded MS70 by today's standards.

Once the banks obtained them, most of these coins were distributed for use as money. However, it was in 1933 that, in the United States, the government melted down most of the coins, and the gold was turned into large bullion that went into the U.S. Gold Reserves.

Thus, very few of these coins, compared to those that were minted, survived in perfect condition, much less in high grades, and it is precisely these that are considered the most valuable; it could be said that they are the great survivors.

You should know that investment coins are scarce coins that have been seen in public offerings very few times. It was in the year 2021 that several auction records were achieved, so the order of the 12 most valuable coins has been slightly modified.

In the case of collectible coins, the characteristics to be considered are a little more different, as they refer to details such as:

- Emission.

- Over-engraved.

- Commemorative.

- Uncirculated coins.

- The year of emission must be considered.

- The material with which it was made.

- The coin must be a different piece.

Fundamental Aspects of Numismatics

Remember that as a discipline, numismatics has a series of formal characteristics to take into account:

- **Antiquarian value:** coins have an intrinsic value beyond their translatable monetary value. They are goods that age and represent historical moments.
- **Notaphilia:** It is not only possible to assess the value of physical coins made of metals. Notaphilia is the numismatic application to elements such as paper money existing in old checks, promissory notes, and banknotes of ancient origin.
- **Scarcity and originality:** Each mint issue throughout history has its particularities. Numismatics brings out the value of such features.
- **Data representation:** Numismatic experts have to represent the real value of a coin considering several aspects: origin, material, conservation, and originality.

What Are Numismatic Collectible Coins?

As I told you in the previous point, numismatic coins have a premium on their precious metal content because they are historic, unique, or have other special qualities that make them rare and valuable. However, it is the context that makes them appealing to collect.

How Do You Calculate the Value of a Numismatic Collectible Coin?
The elements that determine the value of a coin are:

- Conservation over time.

- The intrinsic value.

- The informative content of the events it represents.

- The antiquity of the piece.

- The fashions that are established.

- The number of collectors.

- The information and whims of the people.

These are the most important elements that determine the value of a coin. However, you cannot forget other features that directly influence the value, such as the piece's rarity, scarcity, and demand.

It is also important to analyze that the changes that originated in the coin's value detect two significant variations: those that revalue it and those that devalue it. The former have their origin in fashions, increases in purchasing power, special events, and exotic appreciations by collectors.

Which Coins Are Worth Collecting?

Here are two interesting listings of coins that are worth the investment, time, and study to collect.

A Curated Collection: Highlighting Premier Collectible Coins from the USA, Canada, UK, and Australia

This selection showcases some of the most valuable and sought-after coins currently in circulation within these four major markets, offering unique insights and opportunities for collectors. These coins stand out not only for their historical and monetary value but also for their distinctive features and minting errors that make them exceptionally desirable compared to other global coins.

Valuable Collectible Coins in circulation in the United States.

1. *1970-S Lincoln Cent Doubled Die:*

    Known for its distinct doubling on the obverse elements. This coin shows a strong doubling on the obverse elements. The rare "Small Date" variety is particularly valuable, with approximate values around $3,500 in EF-40 condition.

2. *1972 Lincoln Cent with Doubled Die Obverse:*

    Features strong doubling on all obverse elements. Known for its distinct doubling on all obverse elements, this variety can be worth nearly $500 in EF-40 condition.

3. *2004-D Wisconsin State Quarter with an Extra Leaf:*

    Notable for the extra leaf error. This error coin features an extra leaf on the reverse side. There are High Leaf and Low Leaf varieties, each valued between $200 to $300 in MS-60 condition.

4. *1999 Wide "AM" Reverse Lincoln Cent:*

    This variety shows a clear separation between the letters A and M in "AMERICA" on the reverse. Coins in MS-63 condition can range from $75 to $600, with the 1999 version being the most valuable.

5. *1982 No Mint Mark Roosevelt Dime:*

This dime was struck without a mint mark, making it moderately valuable at about $30 to $50 in AU-50 condition, with higher grades worth more.

6. *The talking coin of John F. Kennedy:*

The former American president was the protagonist of a coin minted by none other than an Asian country, Mongolia. But this is not a coin like any other, but has a button that, when pressed, the phrase said by Kennedy in his 1963 speech in Germany can be heard: "I am a Berliner." These coins were produced in 2007, so although today you can get some of these coins for 50 dollars, not all of them still work.

7. *American Eagle, from the USA:*

It is a 22-karat gold investment coin minted by the United States Mint in 1986 after being approved by the US Congress. The obverse shows the Statue of Liberty wrapped in an American flag. It was redesigned for its 35th anniversary modifying the reverse. Thus, the male flying eagle approaching the nest was replaced by the head of this bird.

8. *American Buffalo, from the USA*

Another of the most popular U.S. Mint investment coins, it was issued in June 2006 and is made of 999.9 thousandths pure gold (24 carats). The obverse features a portrait of a Native American, and the word "freedom" is written on it. The year of mintage also appears in homage to the first inhabitants of that country. The reverse shows a buffalo on top of a mound "as a symbol of the pioneering spirit of the westward expansion of the American nation".

Valuable Collectible Coins in Circulation in the United Kingdom:

9. *2009 Kew Gardens 50p:*

This coin is highly sought after by collectors due to its rarity, with only 210,000 minted.

10. *2012 Olympic Swimming Aquatics 50p:*

One of the early versions of this coin showed waves over the swimmer's head, making it a very desirable piece.

11. *1983 Two Pence "New Pence":*

The version minted in 1983 with the inscription "New Pence" instead of "Two Pence" is extremely rare.

12. *1996 Football European Championship £2:*

This commemorative coin is highly sought after by collectors of sports coins.

13. *2017 Royal Shield £1:*

This coin features a minting error with one side showing the 2016 design and the other side showing the 2017 design, making it a unique and valuable piece.

14. *Queen's Beasts, from the United Kingdom*
This is a series of gold, silver, and platinum coins that began to be issued in 2016 by the Mint of Great Britain and are dedicated to the Queen's Beasts. "Between 2016 and 2021, the Lion of England; the Griffin of Edward III; the Hawk of the Plantagenets; the Black Bull of Clarence; the Yale or Centicore of Beaufort; the White Lion of Mortimer; the White Greyhound of Richmond; the Red Dragon of Wales; the Unicorn of Scotland and the White Horse of Hanover have been issued," they state.

Valuable Collectible Coins in Circulation in Canada:

15. *2000p "Poppy" Quarter:*

The world's first colored coin featuring a red poppy to commemorate Remembrance Day.

16. *1991 "Voyageur" Dollar:*

Minted in limited numbers, it is one of the most sought-after Canadian dollar coins.

17. *1969 Large Date 10 Cent:*

This variant of the 10-cent coin with a large date is very rare and valuable.

18. *1996 "Toonie" with Bear Error:*

This $2 coin has an error in the depiction of the bear, making it highly sought after.

19. *1948 Silver Dollar:*

One of the rarest and most desired coins for Canadian collectors due to its low mintage.

20. *Canadian Maple Leaf*

This coin was created in 1979 by the Government of Canada and minted by the Royal Canadian Mint. "The obverse shows the face of Elizabeth II and the reverse a maple leaf, a tree symbol of this country," they explain. It stands out for its purity of 24 carats, and "it is not alloyed with any other metal".

Valuable Collectible Coins in Circulation in Australia:

21. *2012 Red Poppy $2:*

This commemorative coin is highly sought after for its unique design and limited mintage.

22. *2000 Millennium 50 Cent with Encased Union Flag:*

A rare and valuable coin due to its special design and limited mintage.

23. *2013 Coronation $2:*

Commemorating the coronation of Queen Elizabeth II, this coin holds significant value among collectors.

24. *1988 Bicentennial $2:*

Minted to celebrate Australia's bicentenary, it is highly sought after for its historical significance.

25. *2000 Mule Dollar:*

This $1 coin features a minting error with one side showing a different design, making it extremely rare and valuable.

26. *Chinese Lunar Year, from Australia*

This is a series of pieces issued by the Perth Mint (Australia) since 1996. Each year, these pieces are dedicated to an animal, and 2022 was the turn of the tiger. "Fourteen versions were meant to be minted in 999.9 thousandths gold, platinum (999.5), and silver (999.9)," they detail. The one-ounce version would be limited to 30,000 units.

27. *Australian Nugget*

This coin is manufactured in the two mints of Australia: Perth (Perth Mint) and the Royal Australian Mint (Royal Mint). "The obverse features Queen Elizabeth II, and the reverse features a kangaroo," they explain.

They are composed of 999.9 thousandth pure gold, and the design for 2022 maintains the traditional portrait of the queen on the obverse, while the reverse shows a kangaroo with its calf leaping. "The gold bullion will be available in sizes of one-tenth of an ounce, one-quarter ounce, one-half ounce, one ounce, and one kilogram."

The Most Valuable Collectible Coins in Circulation in the World

Get to know a list of the most valuable coins in the world:

1. Lince, the coin minted in Spain

One of the investment gold coins selected in Spain is the one minted by the Fábrica Nacional de Moneda y Timbre-Real Casa de la Moneda. There is only a limited edition of 12,000 pieces, and it went on sale in December of this year.

It weighs 31.1035 grams, has a purity of 999.9 thousandths, a face value of 1.5 euros, a diameter of 37 millimetres, and a circular shape with a smooth edge. The FNMT-RCM will make an annual series of bullion gold coins available to dealers, collectors, and interested persons.

"The obverse shows the motifs and legends of a "real de a ocho," of columnar type: two hemispheres under a royal crown, flanked by the columns of Hercules with the motto PLUS VLTRA. On the reverse is an image of the head of an Iberian lynx.

2. Krugerrand, from South Africa

This is the investment coin with the highest market share. "It was the first coin issued in the world to contain exactly one ounce of fine gold." It is designed with the popular South African antelope and is composed of an alloy of gold and copper.

It is named after Paul Kruger, a Boer politician who presided over the country in the late 19th century and fought against the United Kingdom. His face is reflected on the obverse and from the rand, the currency of South Africa.

3. Austrian Philharmonic

The Gold Vienna Philharmonic was minted in 1989 by the Austrian Mint in one-ounce and quarter-ounce versions. It is crafted in 999.9 thousandths (24 karats) of pure gold. "It pays tribute to the Vienna Philharmonic Orchestra. Its obverse shows various musical instruments, and its reverse shows the organ in the golden hall of the Vienna Musikverein."

4. 50 pesos

The coin was issued in 1921 in Mexico to honor the centennial of the country's independence from Spain. It has a purity of 999.9 thousandths and weighs 41.6 grams. "90% of its composition is gold, and the remaining 10% is copper". It should be noted that it is one of the most demanded investment coins in the world.

5. Switzerland

This 20-gold franc coin was minted by the Swiss National Mint from 1897-1936 and from 1947-1949. It is composed of 90% gold of 900 thousandths purity". Its obverse features the classic bust of Vreneli, with the Swiss Alps in the background, while the reverse shows the country's coat of arms.

6. The cannabis coin

It was manufactured in Benin, an African country, as part of an edition that had plants as protagonists. This coin has not only the figure of a Cannabis Sativa leaf but also its aroma. Its market value is 90 US dollars.

7. Olympic coins

They were created in Zambia as a way to commemorate the 2000 Olympic Games. The particularity of these coins is that they do not have a circular or geometric shape; perhaps that is why their value in the collector's market is 170 US dollars.

8. The pyramid-shaped coin

The Zambian Olympic coin has not been the only one to break with the circular shape. This time it is a pyramid-shaped creation. This coin was created by the Isle of Man, which is located in the Irish Sea between the islands of Great Britain and Ireland. It has a pyramid shape and is made of copper, and its designs show the death of Tutankhamun, as well as a series of hieroglyphs.

9. The mammoth ivory coin

This coin was created in Ivory Coast, and what makes it so particular is not that it includes the image of an African mammoth but that each of the coins also had a very small portion of fossilized ivory from the animal's tusks. Today, its value on the collector's market is about 117 US dollars.

10. Fiji dollar with meteorite

This is a coin that might seem just a bit extravagant because of its colors, but what makes it part of this particular list is that it has fragments of the Neuschwanstein meteorite! The meteor fell in 2012 on the border of Germany and Austria, and this coin has some small fragments of it on it. Although its value was $10, on the market, it sells for $135.

11. The coin with water

This was issued by one of the islands of Micronesia in 2008 for the 150th anniversary of the apparition of the Virgin of Lourdes in France. The particularity is that it has a small amount of water obtained in the French locality. Like the meteorite coin, this one has a space where you can see the drops of water it contains. Its collector value is 85 US dollars.

12. Kuwaiti Dinar

The Kuwaiti Dinar, currently a currency more than anything else, happens to be one of those hard to get in the market. It is because it is not as widely available as the dollar and the euro. The Kuwaiti Dinar, the Kuwait currency, is subdivided into 1,000 fils. As of 2023, the Kuwaiti dinar is the currency with the highest value per base unit, with KD 1 equivalent to US $ 3.27, ahead of the Bahraini dinar, with BD 1 equivalent to $ 2.65.

It is quite possible that, even if their wealth is recent, many will want to have some of these coins in their collection.

13. Omani Rial

OMR is the currency code for the Omani Rial. It is the national currency of the Sultanate of Oman, a country located on the southeastern coast of the Arabian Peninsula. The Omani rial consists of 1,000 baisas.

Unfortunately, visiting Oman is quite expensive. So, you can start by getting a sample one because having many would require a large investment.

What Are Investment Coins?

Investment coins are known as coins minted in precious metals; generally gold and silver (but also platinum, palladium, and rhodium), not intended for circulation but as a way to store the value of the metals they are made of or as an investment.

Characteristics of Investment Coins

Investment coins usually comply with a series of characteristics that make them be considered "investment pieces." Among the requirements they must meet, we have:

- They must be of a grade equal to or greater than 900 thousandths.

- They must have been minted after 1800.

- They must have been legal tender in their country of origin.

- Currently, they must be traded for a price not exceeding 80% of the market value of the gold contained in them.

- They must be made of precious metals, mainly gold and silver. Therefore, they are issued for investment purposes and not for circulation in the economic environment.

How Is the Value of Investment Coins Calculated?

In addition to the other characteristics that we know give value to a coin, there are others that many people who are entering the world of collecting and investing are unaware of.

The factors that determine the value of investment coins are closely related to supply and demand. This is a basic principle of economics.

The truth is that they must consider details such as the availability of a coin, its condition, and what is the market for that coin at present. All this is precisely what will determine the price to be set. Of course, some factors can increase demand and are sometimes difficult to predict.

The Most Popular Coins for Investors and Collectors

Whether for investing or collecting, some pieces mix the two elements and are commonly sought after by hobbyists. Here are examples of valuable collectible coins currently in circulation for investors and collectors in the USA, Canada, the UK, and Australia.

A. Valuable Collectible Coins in Circulation in the USA:

Flowing Hair ($25,000 or more).

This is a silver dollar coin minted between 1794 and 1795. Although it seems that its life was short, it is one of the most sought-after pieces among collectors.

But this fact is not due to its rarity but to its history, which is linked to the birth of the country and the production of coins.

As for the price, it may cause uncertainty as it has been valued at $25,000 or even more.

10$ Gold Eagle ($5 Million)

If the price of the previous one seemed a bit exaggerated, this piece takes a stratospheric leap. In the year 1804, The Golden Eagle was worth $10, which was the highest denomination until they were discontinued. Only 6 of these coins were produced, of which only 3 exist today.

One is known to have been donated to the American Numismatic Association Museum, and the other two have private individuals.

Here are examples of valuable collectible coins currently in circulation for investors and collectors in the USA, Canada, the UK, and Australia:

The 1850 Silver Dollar ($ 7 million)

Although this coin was produced as early as 1834, collectors did not learn of its existence until 1850, and it was issued only as part of the state's diplomatic mission to Asia.

Due to the small number of coins issued, very few collectors have been able to get their hands on one. Some of these collectors include collector D. Brent Pogue, the Sultan of Muscat, and the Smithsonian Institution. This numismatic treasure has sold for as much as $7,680,000.

Loose Hair Dollar - 1794 ($10 million)

We continue with another silver coin, more specifically with the first one minted by the United States Mint; it was sold in 2013 for $10,016,875 to Bruce Morelan. An estimated 130 examples of this coin still exist, even though 1,758 coins were struck, but many were melted due to poor quality. It was auctioned in October last year without reaching its reserve price.

5$ Gold Coin - 1822 ($8.4 Million)

It became the second most valuable gold coin ever sold, for a sum of $8.4 million; currently, only 3 of these exist and are in private possession.

One of them had been acquired by Virgil Brand in 1899 before Louis Eliasberg bought it in 1945, and then D. Brent Pogue became its owner in 1982.

B. Valuable Collectible Coins in Circulation in Canada:

1936 Dot 10-Cent Coin

This coin is one of the rarest and most valuable Canadian coins, with only five known examples. It features a small raised dot below the date to signify it was minted in 1937. One of these coins sold for $312,000 in 2019.

1921 50-Cent Coin

Known as the "King of Canadian Coins," this coin had an original mintage of 206,398, but most were melted down. Less than 75 examples exist today, and they can fetch between $40,000 to $250,000 at auction (The Collectors Guides Centre) (Gainesville Coins).

C. Valuable Collectible Coins in Circulation in the United Kingdom

2009 Kew Gardens 50p

This coin is highly sought after due to its rarity, with only 210,000 minted. It is one of the most desirable 50p coins among collectors in the UK.

1983 Two Pence "New Pence"

Coins minted in 1983 with the inscription "New Pence" instead of "Two Pence" are extremely rare and valuable, making them highly collectible (The Collectors Guides Centre) (Gainesville Coins).

D. Valuable Collectible Coins in Circulation in Australia:

2012 Red Poppy $2 Coin

This commemorative coin is highly sought after for its unique design and limited mintage. It is one of the most collectible modern Australian coins.

2000 Mule Dollar

Featuring a minting error with a different obverse design, this coin is extremely rare and valuable. It is highly prized by collectors due to its unique error (The Collectors Guides Centre) (Gainesville Coins).

These coins are among the most popular and valuable collectible coins in their respective markets, reflecting their historical significance, rarity, and appeal to collectors and investors alike.

The true price of collectible coins on the market is set by collectors. However, several aspects can affect that value, such as the degree of preservation of the coins, which is usually the most important in determining it.

Silver dollar coins are the most popular. These are highly sought after for their versatility, as they have historical precedent and intrinsic value because they are composed of precious metals.

Some extremely valuable coins have never circulated, while at other times, "normal" coins with certain rarities or errors achieve very high values. Currently, in the United States, there could still be pieces in circulation with this type of "details" that would make such common objects become valuable and unique pieces.

STEP II:

DISCOVER THE SECRETS TO BUILDING A COIN COLLECTION: FIND AND SELECT THE MOST VALUABLE GEMS!

Chapter 3:

How to Recognize a Valuable Coin and Calculate Its Market Value

In this chapter, as a collector, you will learn the best strategies to recognize if a coin is valuable. The idea is that you will acquire all the knowledge provided below and that you will be able to recognize in a short time what you have in your hands.

The Collector-Investor Mentality

The investment industry has changed a lot in the last decade, not only in terms of the securities on offer but also in terms of the profile of the people involved in this world. Little by little, the men in suits and briefcases in hand have been making room for a generation of young people—known as Generation Z—who are moving away from traditional stocks to invest in items with which, in addition to seeing a power of revaluation in the future, they feel culturally and even emotionally connected.

These products range from sneakers to "vintage toys or stickers", which have been working for some years now as alternative and very attractive assets for this audience. This is where coin collecting has gradually come in.

These new forms of investment bring young people closer to a world traditionally associated with more adult people and with a profile linked to finance. However, the last few years have seen a great influx of new sellers. We have seen this trend firsthand, with 70% of our mobile app users under the age of 35 and most of them under the age of 25.

Part of the increase in collection sales is due to product authentication that was previously not guaranteed. Now, the verification mechanisms of both sellers and the objects for sale are exhaustive and guarantee absolute security to the buyer. That is why now, unlike me, you are at a good time to start because you have all the tools to do.

On the other hand, the market for this type of valuables is much more accessible to young people, who may not have the knowledge or interest in complex economic terms, but who do seek a profit for their exclusive sneakers or limited-edition sweatshirt that they have kept safely in their closet for a few years.

Today, around 40% of limited-edition buyers and around 50% of collectors consider the revaluation of the object to be purchased as a fundamental factor when deciding to buy. This is the key to the change of mentality of the new generations and the vision they have when it comes to investing: they are looking for a revaluation of the asset but also for an emotional relationship with the product.

The most interesting point about this situation is that it is tending to improve. Being products of limited collections that cannot be manipulated to maintain their value, when some people buy them to use them, the number of available assets is immediately reduced and, therefore, revalued. The price increases even more when there is no stock left in the stores. But it is not only clothing that triumphs in this new investment model: some young people have earned tens of thousands of dollars selling their NBA players' stickers, and now the new generation of those who collect coins or any other antique objects has arrived.

These series of objects are timeless, completely ingrained in our culture, bring us beautiful memories, and consequently, drive their demand.

Why Buy Only Quality Coins from an Investment Perspective?

Despite having a slightly higher premium than bullion, coins made from precious materials have characteristics that make them superior as an investment tool.

One of the biggest advantages of coins is their greater difficulty in being counterfeited. Because of their particular design, weight, and dimensions, each type of coin contains precise materials that are extremely difficult to replicate.

For some investors, this capital has the advantage that, as most of them are legal tender, they are issued exclusively by national governments.

Finally, the last reason to invest in gold, silver, or other precious coins is their beauty. While bullion coins have a simple and unremarkable appearance, coins are small works of art that can make the eye happy just by looking at them.

Collectible coins, as stated above, can be part of an investment portfolio. You should keep in mind that the value of collectibles does not always respond to market trends and that valuations respond to other factors.

Numismatic collections assume that your goal is to obtain rare coins. The rarer they are, the more valuable they will be. Those who invest in this asset know that, as a business, there can be good returns.

10 Elements to Determine the Value of Collectible Coins

1. *Material*: Coins that can increase their value must be minted in silver. However, they are sold according to the law.

2. *Scarcity*: They must be part of scarce pieces. The year of issue will be the key to being able to sell them more expensive.

3. *Commemorative Issues*: Commemorative coins but in silver. In this case, they would be those that come out for some special celebration because it is the cause that they acquire a numismatic value, in comparison with those that circulate at the moment.

4. *Condition*: Coins that are out of circulation when they are observed in good condition and recently minted could raise their value a little.

5. *Over-engraving*: The over-engraving of some pieces tends to acquire greater value when a date is observed on top of the other.

6. *Uniqueness*: You can determine the characteristic of being a unique piece at the moment if you are a good connoisseur. That is why throughout the book, it is important to emphasize the importance of knowing since anyone who does not understand will overlook details, but not you since you will have the expertise.

7. *Bimetallic Quality*: In bimetallic coins, the assembly of the perimetric ring is practically perfect so that to the touch, no edge can be perceived at its junction with the core or center of the coin.

8. *Edge Details*: The edge can be smooth, striated, discontinuous striated, or with a perimeter groove. If it presents reliefs or other irregularities, it may be a counterfeit coin.

9. *Comparative Examination*: A comparative examination is always necessary and even more so in case of doubts about the authenticity of a coin. It can be compared in its weight, diameter, and thickness with another coin you are sure is genuine. Any difference you notice in weight, diameter, or thickness may indicate that it is a counterfeit coin.

10. *Texture*: The texture of a coin should be smooth. If it feels slippery or soapy, it could be a melted coin and, consequently, a fake coin.

The Slabbing Phenomenon: Why Know About It?

For those just starting with a coin collection, when referring to the slab phenomenon, they must know that this refers to a rolled coin that has been independently authenticated and graded by a certification service. "Slab" is slang for the plastic backing in which the coin is sealed. The most recognized services are PCGS (Professional Coin Grading Service) and NGC (Numismatic Guaranty Corporation).

The slab is made of a specially formed hard acrylic plastic that resists breakage and protects the coin. This encapsulation provides a secure and tamper-evident way to protect the coin from environmental damage and handling. Coins graded by services other than PCGS and NGC are often heavily discounted, as they are typically over-graded or have significant issues.

Even if a coin is properly graded on a slab, it may not be appealing due to unattractive toning or blemishes, and should not be considered for purchase.

The Slabbing Phenomenon in the USA, UK, Canada, and Australia

- *United States*: In the USA, slabbing is a widely accepted practice among collectors and investors. PCGS and NGC are the dominant grading services, providing standardized grading and protection for valuable coins. Examples of highly slabbed and sought-after coins in the USA include the 1909-S VDB Lincoln Cent and the 1916-D Mercury Dime.

- *United Kingdom*: In the UK, slabbing is also gaining popularity among collectors. The most recognized grading service used by UK collectors is the British Numismatic Society (BNS), although PCGS and NGC are widely used here as well. The Royal Mint also provides some degree of certification, especially for commemorative and bullion coins. Grading is crucial for coins such as the 1933 Penny, which is among the rarest British coins.

- *Canada*: In Canada, ICCS (International Coin Certification Service) is a major player in the coin grading market, along with PCGS and NGC. ICCS is known for its strict grading standards, particularly for Canadian coins. Popular collectible coins like the 1948 Silver Dollar are often found slabbed to ensure authenticity and grade.

- *Australia*: Australia's coin collectors primarily rely on PCGS and NGC for their grading needs. The Perth Mint, one of Australia's most renowned mints, issues coins that are frequently submitted for slabbing. The 1930 Penny, one of the most sought-after Australian coins, is often found in slabs to preserve its value and ensure authenticity.

The Slabbing Phenomenon Around the World

- *Europe*: In Europe, slabbing is becoming increasingly popular, especially for high-value and historical coins. Services like NGC and PCGS are widely used. In Germany, the 2002 Silver Proof Euro coins are often slabbed to preserve their condition and verify authenticity. Similarly, in France, the Monnaie de Paris (Paris Mint) issues collectible coins that are frequently sent for grading and slabbing.

- *Asia*: In Asia, coin grading and slabbing have seen a rise in popularity, especially in markets like China and Japan. Chinese Panda coins, particularly the gold and silver issues, are commonly slabbed to protect their value and ensure authenticity. The Japan Mint also issues commemorative coins that are often graded and slabbed by international services like NGC and PCGS to meet the high standards of collectors.

- *South America*: In South America, coin grading is less common but growing in popularity. Countries like Brazil and Argentina have seen an increase in the use of slabbing for collectible coins. Brazilian gold reis and Argentinean silver pesos from the 19th and early 20th centuries are examples of coins that are increasingly sent for professional grading and encapsulation to preserve their condition and enhance their market value.

Coin Grading Standards

Coin grading involves assessing the condition of a coin, which affects its value. The most commonly used grading scale is the Sheldon Scale, ranging from 1 (poor) to 70 (perfect mint state). Here's a brief overview of the grading standards in the USA, UK, Canada, and Australia:

United States:

- *Penny*: One cent
  1 cent ($0.01): Penny - One cent
- *Nickel*: Five cents
  5 cents ($0.05) Nickel - Five cents
- *Dime*: Ten cents
  10 cents ($0.10) Dime - Ten cents
- Quarter: Twenty-five cents
  25 Ents ($0.25) Quarter - Twenty-Five cents
- *Half Dollar*: Fifty cents
  50 Ents ($ 0.50) Half dollar (not widely used) - Fifty cents
- *Dollar*: One dollar
  1 dollar ($1.00) One dollar

United Kingdom

- *Farthing*: 1/4 penny (no longer in circulation)
- *Penny*: One penny
- *Tuppence*: Two pence
- *Threepence*: Three pence
- *Sixpence*: Six pence
- *Shilling*: Twelve pence
- *Florin*: Two shillings

- *Half Crown*: Two shillings and sixpence
- *Crown*: Five shillings

Canada

- *Penny*: One cent (no longer minted)
- *Nickel*: Five cents
- *Dime*: Ten cents
- *Quarter*: Twenty-five cents
- *Half Dollar*: Fifty cents
- *Dollar*: One dollar
- *Toonie*: Two dollars

Australia

- *Penny*: One penny (pre-decimal, no longer in circulation)
- *Threepence*: Three pence (pre-decimal)
- *Sixpence*: Six pence (pre-decimal)
- *Shilling*: Twelve pence (pre-decimal)
- *Florin*: Two shillings (pre-decimal)
- *Decimal Penny*: One cent (no longer in circulation)
- *Nickel*: Five cents
- *Dime*: Ten cents
- *Twenty Cent*: Twenty cents
- *Fifty Cent*: Fifty cents
- *Dollar*: One dollar
- *Two Dollar*: Two dollars

Ways to Calculate the Coins' Market Value

Understanding the market value of your coins is crucial for both beginners and advanced collectors. Here are various methods to accurately determine the value of your coins, with tips and tricks for collectors in the USA, UK, Canada, and Australia

1. **Using Specialized Auction Indexers**

If you have not found your coin in *coleccionistasdemonedas.com*, do not despair, there is another method to know its price. Specialized auction indexers are a great source of information due to their rigour and continuous updating. Here you have a *step-by-step* guide to use them without dying in the attempt.

- *Search by Keyword*: Enter specific keywords related to your coin. For example, if you have a Roman macrine denarius, type this into the search box.
- *Subscription Services*: Some platforms require a subscription (about $75 a year) to see detailed pricing. However, you can often get price information from other free sources.
- *Find Similar Coins*: Look for coins of a similar type and state of conservation. This will give you a good reference for the current market value if the auction date is recent.
- *Auction Details*: Note the auction company name, auction number, and lot number.
- *Aggregator Websites*: Use powerful aggregators of old coin auctions to know the real value that the coin reached at auction. These usually contain references to auctions in the United States, the rest of America, Europe, and beyond.

Useful Tips for Collectors:

- USA: Use platforms like Heritage Auctions and Stack's Bowers for comprehensive auction data.
- UK: Try Baldwin's Auctions and The London Coin Company for local auction results.
- Canada: Check with Torex Coin Show and Auction, and Colonial Acres for Canadian coin values.
- Australia: Look at Noble Numismatics and Downies for auction prices in the Australian market.

2. Using Apps to Calculate the Value of Old Coins in Your Home

Possibly this method is the least effective since, on many occasions, the indicative prices are not correct. These apps use the image search method.

In practically all our tests with these mobile applications, the result has been unsatisfactory: many prices are missing, the ones they offer are outdated, and the images in their database do not match the state of conservation of our coin.

They work as follows:

First, you must take a photo of the coins with very good quality, correct lighting, and adequate zoom to ensure sufficient sharpness. Once this is done, it is checked against a database of coin images with prices, and you must choose the one that best suits your coin.

The main drawback is that its percentage of accuracy concerning the type of coin is high, but concerning its grading, it is low. That means that the orientation price it offers you may have nothing to do with reality.

The main apps are **Coinoscope** and **Maktun**. Coinoscope is known for high accuracy in identifying coin types, but less reliable for grading. Maktun is similar to Coinoscope but has the same drawbacks regarding grading accuracy. As I said, they have more disadvantages than advantages, so in our opinion, they are not recommended.

3. Catalogs of Ancient Coins

Sometimes catalogs are not good references. You will understand it perfectly taking into account these reasons:

- They are incomplete: not only are many rare coins missing but sometimes even very common coins at auctions are also omitted.

- The value of old coins moves: While the price of coins changes over time, the price of catalogs does not.

In some cases, publishers manipulate prices according to what they are interested in selling: it is common to put low prices on expensive coins and high prices on cheap coins. The difference between the catalog and auction values can be up to 500%.

4. Online Resources and Price Guides

Websites like Numista, PCGS Price Guide, and NGC Coin Explorer offer extensive databases and price guides that are frequently updated. These can be highly reliable sources for understanding coin values.

5. Joining Numismatic Societies and Forums

Joining numismatic societies or online forums can provide access to exclusive information and expert opinions. Societies like the American Numismatic Association (ANA), the British Numismatic Society (BNS), and the Royal Canadian Numismatic Association (RCNA) offer valuable resources and networking opportunities.

Chapter 4:

Strategies for Learning the System That Makes the Coin Market Profitable

When you are involved in a business like this, you must be an over-analyzer: you must examine the best strategies to understand the system that makes the currency market profitable, even if you don't have much time in it. You will learn about it in this chapter.

The Best Coin Investing Strategies: How to Quickly Understand the System That Makes the Coin Market Profitable

Investing in art objects, vintage vehicles, stamps, and, in short, any type of collectible good consists of buying unique or existing objects in very few units in the hope that, in the future, they will increase in value. It is an investment that can be very profitable, but it is not risk-free.

Below, we summarize the main advantages and disadvantages of investing in collectibles and tell you which objects have historically been appreciated the most.

It can be a very profitable investment, more so than a conventional investment fund or the purchase of shares, for example.

There are few experts in the field, so competition is reduced, and if you are an expert in some kind of collectible, you can find good opportunities.

You can enjoy the assets you invest in. If you spend on a painting, a sculpture, or some coins, in addition to an investment, they will be an object of personal enjoyment for you and your loved ones.

One of the biggest fears for new and advanced collectors is the potential devaluation of their collections. To mitigate this risk:

- *Research Thoroughly*: Always research the coin's historical value and current market trends. Use reputable sources such as the PCGS Price Guide, NGC, and auction house records.
- *Focus on Quality*: High-quality coins, even in turbulent markets, tend to retain or increase their value. Prioritize coins in excellent condition with clear provenance.
- *Diversify Your Collection*: Just as with any investment portfolio, diversification can protect against significant losses. Include coins from different periods, regions, and types.

Understanding the coin market quickly is essential for busy collectors:

- *Use Trusted Resources*: Utilize reliable resources like coin grading services (PCGS, NGC) and reputable auction houses (Heritage Auctions, Stack's Bowers). These provide accurate valuations and market insights.
- *Join Numismatic Societies*: Organizations like the American Numismatic Association (ANA), the British Numismatic Society, and the Royal Canadian Numismatic Association offer valuable information and networking opportunities.
- *Leverage Technology*: Use apps and online platforms to get real-time updates and valuations. Apps like Coinoscope can provide quick insights, through cross-reference with established guides for accuracy.

How to Obtain Excellent Yields by Generating Profits with Your Coins

The financial yield, therefore, is the profit that a certain operation allows you to obtain. It is a calculation made by taking the investment made and the profit generated after a certain period. In other words, the financial yield relates the profit achieved to the resources employed.

1. *Prioritize the implementation of a strategic plan*

Strategic planning is an activity that studies all the corporate areas of a company, thus making it possible to prioritize the essential tasks for its operation.

For this reason, defining objectives and analyzing the reality of the financial sector is essential to optimize decision-making. Indeed, before taking any action, it is necessary to verify whether the organization has sufficient financial resources to meet not only its recurring obligations but also to embrace new projects.

2. *Implement tools that make management easier*

It is important to understand that technological innovation has brought incredible and numerous benefits to the financial area.

For this reason, the company must incorporate specific software that centralizes information, thus ensuring that managers can have a broader view of finances and make better decisions.

Nowadays, it is possible to find an endless number of management software options to control cash, receipts and disbursements, payments, obligations, and contracts, among other activities.

To select a good solution for your business, it is necessary to identify your requirements and verify which alternative is most suitable for your company.

3. *Train the work team*

One of the main pillars of efficient financial management is to have a skilled and trained work team to act in any scenario and offer excellent results.

Under this vision, the company must carry out training instances with new and updated content that contributes to the work activity.

It is even advisable to participate in these moments of interaction since they make it possible to get to know the employees better and understand their needs and expectations.

Likewise, adequate team training favors productivity and promotes the employees' proactivity. In this sense, it is essential to stimulate their autonomy by delegating functions and tasks that allow them to make decisions without consulting their superiors.

In other words, the manager must create an environment that allows employees to act on their own, thus reducing corporate bureaucracy.

4. Monitor the market

The relationship between the company and the customer is often volatile. This means that nowadays, a very interesting, effective, and sought-after solution can lose ground and become obsolete in a short space of time.

As a result, a brand can significantly reduce the number of sales and customers, thus generating the idea of being weak and outdated in the face of competition.

Based on this scenario, it is easy to understand why it is so relevant to monitor the market. When the company keeps its eyes and ears open for updates, it can detect novelties in technological, social, cultural, and behavioral terms.

In this way, it has the means to act quickly and ensure that its solutions maintain attractive features, benefits, and advantages for customers and generate good revenues for the company.

In addition, understanding market behavior is fundamental to projecting your company's performance and aligning revenues to corporate costs, thus avoiding a lack of financial resources.

5. Analyze results

Being attentive to the business results allows for understanding which strategies and actions are bringing good profits and making it possible to identify errors and failures in management.

Therefore, it is essential to keep strict control of sales, investments, debts, and all aspects that may, in one way or another, have an impact on the financial performance of the business. In this way, it is possible to optimize decision-making and ensure the creation of emerging measures following corporate needs.

6. Set aside part of the profit for investment

Creating an investment culture is an important step to improve the financial picture. Indeed, if you manage to set aside part of the profits to invest in the business, whether for training, buying equipment, or offering new products or services, you can add value to the brand and obtain a better position in the market.

This leads to increased revenue and, therefore, improved corporate profitability.

In addition to setting aside an amount for investment, you must maintain and nurture an emergency financial reserve to ensure working capital and the survival of the collecting business in the event of an unfavorable economic situation.

Likewise, you have an amount to face unexpected situations. It avoids resorting to loans to meet the payment of simple operations and reflects a solid and secure image before the market players.

After all, you have read, you will already know that improving the management of financial resources before investing is not an excessively complex task. However, to succeed in the mission, you should keep these tips in mind, apply them and measure their effectiveness by comparing the corporate situation before and after the implementation of the strategies.

How to Participate in Collectible Auctions and Learn the Strategies of the Best Coin Collectors

Most auction house advertisements use the standard auction format. Standard auctions work as follows:

- *Understand the Auction Process*: Familiarize yourself with how auctions work, including the bidding process and auction formats.
- *Set a Budget*: Determine your maximum bid beforehand to avoid overspending.
- Research the Coins: Study the coins up for auction, focusing on their history, condition, and market value.
- *Use Online Platforms*: Many auctions are now online, allowing you to participate from anywhere. Platforms like eBay, Heritage Auctions, and Stack's Bowers are excellent places to start.
- *Network with Other Collectors*: Engage with other collectors to gain insights and share strategies.

How to Generate Profits and Monetize with Collectible Coins

To give you an idea, the average increase in starting prices of all coins until recently has registered an increase of 85%. In addition, the average percentage of lots sold at auction houses is one of the highest in the market, reaching 98.3% this year.

When it comes to more specialized collectors, they opt for more exclusive pieces. The truth is that the sale of collections of coins or a single specimen shows that just by being a rare good, the ancient coin is presented as an exemplary and unique exclusivity.

Does this mean that anyone without previous knowledge of numismatics can invest in historical coins? Yes, but it is important to turn to professionals who can provide the necessary advice according to particular circumstances.

The amount to start acquiring a small numismatic heritage is not something that requires a large investment. There are cases of people with less exclusive pieces that involve investments of less than $1,000. What happens in the vast majority of situations is that they progressively feel more confident to bid for more outstanding pieces.

In short, numismatics is a booming tangible asset, an economic refuge in uncertain times that provides stability, confidence, and flexibility to the saver, as well as the added attraction of owning exclusive objects that have survived history for hundreds or even thousands of years.

Turn Your Collection into an Investment Asset by Relying on Quality Instead of Quantity

When talking about investing, you need to understand that there are different types of financial investments. While these are meant to earn returns for the investor, they are not a guaranteed way to receive them. Different types of investment allow for different forms of earnings, which is why when talking about currencies, the idea or goal is to focus on having an asset that offers quality.

As in any type of business, there is a risk that, instead of profits, the investor may obtain losses. It should be noted that investments have two key qualities that are directly related: profitability and risk.

In an investment, whether in currencies or any other asset, the higher the risk associated with it, the higher its profitability may be. This is something you should not forget in finance, the greater the promise of income, the greater the possibility of risk, and vice versa, relatively reliable investments where the risk is low or very calculated never allow you to count on high profits.

You should know that there is a great tendency to earn in a collector's coin or investment because, as mentioned before, the market of collector's coins has increased exponentially. More and more people want to enter, either because they see it as a business or just because they are interested in belonging to a group specialized in this hobby, and the stories of the coins attract them.

Tips for American, British, Canadian, and Australian Collectors

United States	United Kingdom	Canada	Australia
Join the American Numismatic Association (ANA): They offer extensive resources, educational programs, and a platform for buying and selling coins.	Connect with the British Numismatic Society: They offer detailed resources on British coins and host events for collectors.	Royal Canadian Numismatic Association (RCNA): Offers resources and networking opportunities for Canadian collectors.	Australasian Numismatic Dealers Association (ANDA): Offers resources and networking for Australian collectors.
Use Platforms Like Heritage Auctions and Stack's Bowers: These auction houses provide valuable market insights and auction opportunities.	Spink & Son Auctions: One of the oldest coin dealers in the UK, providing a wide range of British and world coins.	Use Colonial Acres for Transactions: A well-known platform for buying and selling Canadian coins.	Participate in Noble Numismatics Auctions: A reputable auction house for Australian and world coins.

STEP III:

THE ULTIMATE GUIDE TO COIN INVESTING: HOW TO BUY, SELL, AND PROFIT FROM RARE COINS

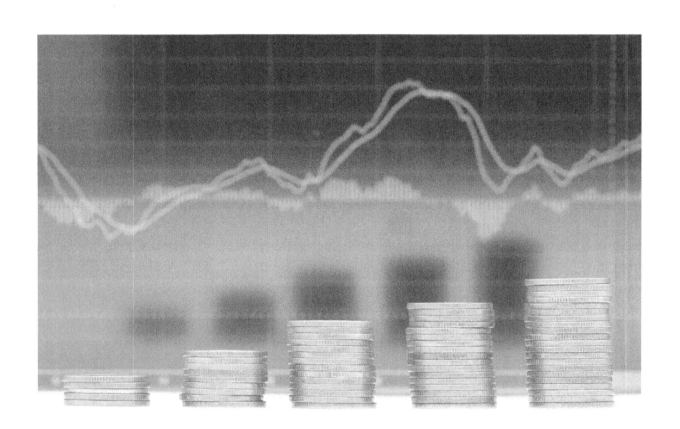

Chapter 5: Buying and Selling Coins

In this chapter, you will learn some tips that you may not have been told about buying and selling coins and the details you should take care of when you are about to buy or sell a piece. Also, the different options of places you can count on to identify the market and, with it, a series of recommendations that you should use as a buyer and seller to avoid scams.

The Best Strategies Used by Coin Collectors to Buy and Sell Successfully

Here we present a series of tips that are more like the strategies that you should adopt and use and that will help you to handle the buying and selling of coins like an expert since we all have to deal with it at some point when it starts:

1. *Consult Experts*: when it comes to investigating your coin's value, you should know that the most advisable thing to do is not to go in the first instance to sell your coins in a numismatic house. It is recommended that you consult the experts of these houses and that they guide you as to an idea of the price.

    This process is very similar to when you go to pawn an object; you should know that you will usually be offered less money than what your old coins are worth. Otherwise, the owners of these places would not be able to make a profit when it comes to finding an end customer. However, they can give you an approximate price for the value of your coin.

2. *Clear Descriptions*: as for a strategy you should employ to sell a coin, you need to describe your piece clearly, simply, and correctly. It should be a description that specifically highlights why your coin is special and why they should buy it at a good price.

3. *High-Quality Photos*: opt for high-quality photos because no matter how beautiful, attractive, and unique your coins are, or even if it is the most expensive coin in the world, no one will buy it if you do not give it a good presentation.

4. *Sales Strategy*: determine the best sales strategy. Whether by lots or individually, you must choose how to sell your old coins to get the best price. For example, some commemorative 20-peso coins belong to the same collection, although they are different from each other. Here it would be convenient to sell each coin separately because each one of them may be the missing piece of several collections. Then, even if you have them repeated, they can be worth much more if you sell them to someone who needs them urgently.

5. *Avoid Resellers* because they are attentive and will always offer you the lowest price to make a profit later. Instead, identify the real collectors.

6. *Safe Transactions*: do not forget to choose public places in case you have to make a delivery in person; try to make it in crowded and guarded places.

7. *Attend Numismatic Events*: go to numismatic events in your city because it is common that there you will find real collectors, those who will know how to appreciate your most valuable coins.

Tips and Tricks for Buying and Selling Rare Coins

If you have or wish to buy rare coins, you should first know that a large number of collectors are looking to buy and sell their coins in the country.

When it comes to selling and buying, the good news is that currently, the market is plagued with many who would pay a great price for them, and it is precisely in those places that you can also find the pieces you are looking for.

To be safe, you should know that many companies conduct auctions in person or online and that you can enter for free.

In the web portals that exist to disseminate information on antique coin auctions, you can also find those coins that you may have trouble finding. All you have to do is search by location, and the options will surely appear.

When it comes to buying and selling rare coins, consider these tips:

- *Auction Participation*: Many companies conduct auctions in person or online. These platforms are often the best places to find and sell rare coins.
- *Research*: Use web portals that disseminate information on antique coin auctions. They can help you find rare coins that are hard to come by.
- *Verify Sellers*: Ensure that the sellers or auction houses you are dealing with are reputable and have good reviews.

Differences and Similarities for Buying and Selling Investment Coins

If you are going to buy or sell your investment coins, you must be clear about a series of discrepancies and avoid mistakes in the buying and selling process.

These differences and similarities are evident in both processes since both involve a transaction.

- In the purchase of currency, you are going to invest money to acquire a piece that is considered unique or special, while in the sale, you get a profit for your special product, and you must offer a quality piece.

  Similarities: In either case, special attention to the transaction steps and processes is required.

- A collection of silver or gold coins is a means of investment and a haven used by more and more people every day. Therefore, you must pay special attention to the details that make the difference, such as the material of your piece.

  Discrepancies: When it comes to selling an asset of this type, you must be especially cautious not to fall into scams because, from the moment you have this type of coin, you know that you are more prone to theft or robbery.

- It is possible that before selling, you have already gone through the buying process, which is why you should know that when you sell collectible coins, you should apply a series of strategies.

Mistakes to Avoid When Buying and Selling Coins

Here are a series of mistakes to avoid that many people make when it comes to buying and selling coins:

Buying in Any Establishment Without First Verifying its Origin

Several stores are dedicated specifically to numismatics; it is advisable to search for them precisely with this term in the first instance. There you can find real objects whose valuation has been established by an expert on the subject.

Avoid internet sites or informal purchases, as they could sell you an item not worth its cost.

Misinformation

If there is one thing that the art of coin collecting refers to, it is the fact that the collector is a connoisseur of the piece.

If you are interested in buying coins and starting your collection, you need to learn about the subject. Learn about the characteristics of the coins, their history, their cultural impact, and so on. The more you learn, the harder it will be to fall for fraud. In addition, you will be able to recognize valuable pieces more easily.

Later on, you will find a series of resources, such as magazines that you can consult and where you will find more details and information about coins.

Too High Expectations When Selling Coins

This is one of the most common mistakes. It makes sense when thousands of articles on the internet promise that "you can become a millionaire by selling that old coin you have in a drawer in your house." It's almost impossible for anything like that to happen.

Most collectible antique coins are worth less than 100 euros or dollars. Only rare, well-preserved specimens can fetch thousands of dollars or euros.

I recommend you level the odds and consult a numismatic specialist to know the real value of your old coin.

Selling Without Knowing the Price of the Coin Individually or in Batches

Antique coins can be sold in batches of many coins, or specific specimens can be sold individually. Selecting one way or the other depends on several factors, such as the rarity of the coin, the state of conservation, the offer price, and the existing demand, among others. Therefore, before publishing, establish the price you calculated.

Each way has its pros and cons. When you have a very rare and valuable specimen that many collectors would like to have, it is better to sell it individually. This way, all the attention is focused on the piece, and there are no other issues that can divert attention.

On the other hand, lots of old coins usually have specimens of different types, grades, and prices. One lot may have two or three very valuable and in-demand coins, and another group, more common and less valuable coins.

Being a sale by the lot, those interested in the valuable coins are obliged to buy them all to get the ones they are interested in. So, you must know these details before publishing.

Selling Motivated by a Need

Suppose you have a unique, well-preserved piece, and a specialist has told you that you can sell it very expensively. The last thing you should do is try to sell it to solve money problems.

If you decide to sell your coins because you are struggling with money or because you want to buy something very expensive, chances are that a buyer will sense your desperation and try to take advantage by offering you less money than the real value of your piece.

Selling in a Hurry

The market for old coins is quite active, but it is not as dynamic as other types of collectibles. People who buy antique coins for collecting like to take precautions to be certain about the pieces they are acquiring.

Before buying, they usually get well informed about the type of coin and the particular specimen when there are records of it. Showing haste in the sale can send incorrect signals that will make them more cautious and hesitate.

How to Check the Condition and Quality of Coins

To begin with, I would like to clarify that if you require an accurate valuation of your coins, it is best to take them to a numismatic appraiser.

If, on the other hand, you are satisfied with an approximate valuation, you should know a few methods:

1. *Official Catalogs*: you can go to sites frequented by numismatists, such as the United States Mint and other official coin sites, to obtain the official catalogs and manuals for selling coins.

2. *Auction Indexers*: the second method is to turn to specialized auction indexers. The third method is to go to eBay and look under "Coins and Banknotes," go to "search

including," and then check "Sold listings." In the "Sort by" field, select "End date: most recent first." Finally, search for coins similar to the one you own.

3. *Online Marketplaces*: another method is to search by images in specialized applications such as Coinoscope and Maktun, although the results are usually quite indicative.

What Precautions to Take

In this section, I will give you several tips so that you are not like the people who ask for exorbitant amounts for their collections. They do it because most of the time, what happens is that they are confused about the true value of the pieces since they believe that they keep objects that could reach millionaire figures when in fact it is not so.

- Several places can guide you on prices and where you can find out if collectors would pay a high cost for your product, but you have to be careful because scams in this type of trade are very common.

- Be sure to seek the opinion and valuation of an expert, as this is the most reliable source of information. You can also visit museums where there are surely trained personnel in these areas.

How to Display Your Coin Collection [coin display label, etc.].

When it comes to displaying your coin collections, the possibilities are vast. Here are some of the most common methods:

Albums

Albums are specifically designed to display coins. Ring binders with generic plastic sheets may be an option to consider, especially if you like the album system but don't want to compress previous collections.

Coin Trays

These are usually made of plastics specifically designed for preservation; collectors with high-value pieces often use trays as they offer greater protection than the other cases.

The benefits of using coin trays are that they include different compartments with different sizes and offer a more enjoyable way to display coins.

Coin Books

This is undoubtedly the most common option that you can make yourself, and it is also one of the most used by those who are new to numismatics. The reasons? The market offers products specifically for them, for example, albums to keep coins in which the classification by year or country is already included.

Among the disadvantages is the fact that by including the grading, you may run the risk of not having enough space for other "extras" you may need.

Mylar Cardboard

You may not have heard of this option, but it is a very popular alternative for coin collectors and is the classic square cardboard with a thin plastic in the center, designed to make the coin visible.

Without a doubt, this is a very interesting way to protect the coins; it is an economical material and allows you to display them.

How, Where, and When It Is More Convenient to Buy and Sell Your Coins for Profits

Coin collectors are indeed all over the world. However, this community is very strong in the United States and some European countries.

This is why it pays to know where you can sell in the United States. If you are in a hurry, many auction houses and pawnshops will be willing to buy your old coin.

Remember that these places will offer you less money than the real value of the piece since they will sell it at a higher price to make a profit.

Some cities where you are likely to get a good price are New York, Los Angeles, California, and Miami. These places have large and established communities of coin collectors who are always eager to buy pieces to add to their collections.

You can also go to Houston, Dallas, or Chicago, although in these places, the collecting communities are smaller.

Selling Coins on eBay

It is possible to sell various types of coins on eBay by creating a free seller account and generating listings for each coin you wish to offer.

It is important to consider aspects such as managing coin listings, which should include images of the coins, a description of their condition, and details about their history and background.

The important point is that you are aware that this is an alternative that presents certain risks and is classified as less professional than others, so it is recommended to be very careful if you are a beginner in this area of selling.

The steps:

1. The first step to selling coins on eBay is to create a seller account, which requires choosing a username and password and verifying an email address.

2. Once you have created a merchant account, place your credit card on file, link a verified PayPal account to your merchant account, and maintain a minimum level of merchant performance. You can open an online store.

3. While stores are not required to sell on the site, they can be convenient, as they offer a centralized location for all your listings and give you the ability to brand your online sales.

4. Regardless of the selling method chosen, all items sold on eBay require an individual listing consisting of images of the item, a description, and a selling method.

5. You can implement a traditional auction model or place a "Buy It Now" price that allows buyers to bypass the auction option and purchase the coin immediately.

The Perfect Time to Sell Your Coins

These days it seems easier to sell coins thanks to websites, but the ease doesn't mean that any time is the perfect one. However, coin collectors know that the two best seasons of the year to sell coins are the FUN show in January and the summer ANA from July through August.

These are the best periods to sell and buy coins on your own, on consignment, or through a US auction. You are more likely to get the best prices when people are in a good mood to buy coins.

Where to Find Collectible Coins?

If you're wondering where you can find coins, then start with these places:

Numismatic Store

Commonly, at this type of place, you can get a fair quote and learn a little more about the business while you shop. As a suggestion, visit several numismatic stores until you get the one that offers you the best price for your coins.

Physical Auction

You can also opt for a physical auction by contacting a reputable numismatic auction house. Auction houses usually have unique pieces.

Online Auction

On the Internet, there are online auction modalities where collectors can find unique coin pieces.

Collectors' Websites

It is thanks to the popularity of numismatics that collectors have come to form groups of fair coin markets for auctions and sales, an excellent option to find the pieces you are looking for.

- Great Collections: This site offers one of the best series of options for ancient coins.

- Apmex: This is a well-known site that operates a business model similar to pawnshops. It has competitive prices and fixed prices.

- Teletrade: In addition to offering special pieces, it also offers some of the best shipping options.

- Heritage Auctions: It is one of the leading collectibles sites in the United States, and that is reflected in its earnings of more than a billion dollars a year from the sale of very valuable items. Here you can easily find your collectible coins.

- Modern Coin Mart: It also works similarly to a pawnshop, where you can usually find any piece, just keep in mind that it may be at a high cost.

Note: Later in Chapter 8 you will find a list of links to places where you can find antique or investment coins.

The Best Physical Locations for a Coin Collector

Check out these options that you can visit and learn about if you are looking for ancient coins:

1. Banking institutions

When it comes to looking for that special coin, it is a good idea to visit a bank near your place of residence; some of them usually have pieces for sale.

2. Auction houses

Auction houses are the main places to visit when a collector is looking for an antique coin. However, you should be prepared, as many of them are looking for the same thing as you and usually make juicy offers that exceed your budget.

3. Numismatic houses

Before visiting numismatic houses, find out what kind of coins they sell and what you want to get; remember the characteristics that the piece must have.

4. Pawnshops

Pawnshops will always be a place where they usually have objects that you never imagined, and they may have those coins you never imagined, so it is a good idea to visit these places and check them out.

5. Gold and silver houses

In these places, you can run with luck to find collector's coins because these are the places that have these types of coins.

6. Mercaditos

As is well known, neighborhood markets or the famous garage sales that are so popular in some countries are excellent places to acquire old coins at relatively low prices.

So if you are beginning coin collecting, you need to know that old coins can be purchased at flea markets. This is an excellent way to get started in the world of coin collecting without making a large investment.

7. State Fairs

At the fun annual convention in Fort Lauderdale, you can find several options for recent coins, ancient coins, medals, heritage auctions, and all types of numismatics.

8. International numismatic events in Chicago

The international events held at the Donald E. Stephens Convention Center in Rosemont, Chicago, Illinois, USA, are an ideal place to look for your coins.

9. United States Mint in Philadelphia, Pennsylvania

This internationally recognized coin mint has a gift store where you can browse through its coin collection options.

10. Antique stores

These stores offer prices that are commensurate with the coins, plus they have a knowledgeable staff to assist you. They master the characteristics of the objects so they can locate the piece you are looking for.

The Best Websites for a Coin Collector

If there is something to thank for the new technologies is that buyers now have online places to make their purchases. These websites offer catalogs and detailed information about the coins for sale as if you saw them in person. You just have to verify that they are official portals or stores to avoid scams. However, this list will surely be of great help and guidance:

Specialized USA Coin Sites

Newman Numismatic Portal
The Newman Numismatic Portal is located at Washington University in St. Louis and is funded by the Eric P. Newman Numismatic Education Society. The NNP is dedicated to becoming the leading and most comprehensive resource for numismatic research and reference material, initially concentrating on U.S. coins.

NGC World Price Guide

Numismatic Guaranty Company (NGC ®) is the world's largest and most trusted third-party coin, token, and medal grading service. Starting from 1987, NGC has graded more than 55 million coins, each of them backed by the industry-leading NGC Guarantee.

The United States Mint

The United States Mint is a bureau of the Department of the Treasury responsible for producing coins for the United States to conduct commerce and control the movement of bullion. It does not produce paper money since this activity is entrusted to the Bureau of Engraving and Printing.

PCGS Coin Facts

This is a detailed online encyclopedia of U.S. coins. As the most comprehensive database of U.S. coins on the Internet, CoinFacts is the main educational resource for people to buy, sell, and collect coins.

CoinFacts includes historical narratives to help you learn about the pieces you love, accompanied by relevant and up-to-date information on the value of collectible coins.

Great Collections Inc

This site offers some of the best commission rates for selling old coins. If you sell an item for a price of $1,000, they charge you 0%; if the price is less than $1,000, the fee is just 5%. Also, since 2013 it has been the ideal site for storage and grading and a good marketplace for valuable coins.

Coin news.net

It is a portal for daily coin news, articles, and updates on coins and collecting, with free resources for collectors, such as coin pricing.

PCGS

Professional Coin Grading Service is the Internet's leading site for coin collectors. It has numismatic experts who can advise you.

It is a world leader in coin grading and authentication services, guaranteed. It offers a coin price guide, population reports, and rare and modern coin data.

Mint Error News

The Mint Error News website has become the most popular and informative online resource on mint errors and is read by thousands of dealers and collectors.

American Numismatic Association

The American Numismatic Association is an organization founded in 1891 by George Francis Heath. Located in Colorado Springs, Colorado, it was formed to advance the knowledge of numismatics along educational, historical, and scientific lines and increase interest in the hobby.

Additional Suggested Sites for American Numismatics:

Heritage Auctions

- Service: Leading auction house for coins and collectibles.
- Website: Heritage Auctions https://www.ha.com/

Stack's Bowers Galleries

- Service: Auctions and sales of rare coins and paper money.
- Website: Stack's Bowers https://stacksbowers.com/

Specialized UK Coin Sites

The Royal Mint

The official source for British coin information and current releases.

royalmint.com

Coin Yearbook

A reference guide with current UK coin values.

coinyearbook.co.uk

London Coin Auctions

Offers auctions specializing in British coins with online catalogs.

londoncoins.co.uk

Spink & Son

One of the oldest and most respected coin dealers in the UK, offering a wide range of British and world coins.

spink.com

Specialized Canadian Coin Sites

Royal Canadian Mint

The official source for Canadian coin information and current releases.

www.mint.ca

Colonial Acres Coins

Offers a wide range of Canadian coins and numismatic supplies, with regular auctions and online shopping.

colonialacres.com

Canadian Coin & Currency

A leading dealer in Canadian coins, offering a vast selection of rare and collectible coins.

canadiancoin.com

J&M Coin and Jewellery

Based in Vancouver, this site offers a comprehensive selection of Canadian coins and banknotes.

jandm.com

Coins Unlimited

Serving collectors with a wide selection of Canadian coins and numismatic supplies, as well as regular auctions.

coinsunlimited.ca

Specialized Australian Coin Sites

The Perth Mint

The official source for Australian coin information and current releases.

perthmint.com

Downies

A major dealer in Australian coins, offering a wide range of numismatic products and online auctions.

downies.com

Royal Australian Mint

The official mint of Australia, providing information on current and historical coin releases.

ramint.gov.au

Coinworks

Specializing in rare and historical Australian coins, offering a selection of high-quality numismatic items.

coinworks.com.au

Sterling & Currency

Offers a wide range of Australian coins, banknotes, and numismatic supplies, with an online catalog.

sterlingcurrency.com.au

These specialized sites provide comprehensive resources for coin collectors and investors in the USA, UK, Canada, and Australia, offering valuable information, market prices, and avenues for buying and selling coins.

The Best Applications

In addition to the aforementioned portals, you can also download several apps from your mobile and thus begin to learn more about coins. These are:

USA-Specific Applications

Maktun

Maktun is a new free application for numismatists, coin collectors, and note-takers. It is suitable for both beginners and experienced collectors.

In Maktun, you can identify a coin and a banknote from a phone photo and know about 300 thousand types of coins.

PCGS CoinFacts - U.S. Coin Val

U.S. coin collectors finally have the resource they need to make informed numismatic buying, selling, and trading decisions, thanks to the PCGS CoinFacts mobile app.

It's the world's largest encyclopedia of U.S. coins that now fits in your pocket and is 100% free. Just download this coin-collecting mobile app today to access coin values, images, narratives, auction prices, and much more for over 39,000 U.S. coins.

COINage

COINage has been a leading name in numismatic publications, and to make its service bigger and broader, they offer a new perspective on numismatics for the experienced coin collector and an introduction to key concepts for the novice.

The goal of the app is to provide informative and entertaining articles for these audiences and to attract new people to the hobby, making it ideal if you are at an intermediate level of learning numismatics.

UK-Specific Applications

Change Checker

Change Checker is a popular app among UK coin collectors, allowing users to track their collections, swap coins with other collectors, and access up-to-date coin information and values.

Website: Change Checker https://www.changechecker.org/

Coinoscope

Coinoscope is an image recognition app that helps identify coins by taking a photo. It includes information on UK coins and is handy for both novice and experienced collectors.

Website: Coinoscope https://coinoscope.com/

Canadian-Specific Applications

Coins of Canada

Coins of Canada provides detailed information about Canadian coins, including values, mintages, and images. It is a valuable resource for collectors of Canadian numismatics.

Website: Coins of Canada https://www.coinsofcanada.com/

Canadian Coin

This app offers a comprehensive catalog of Canadian coins, providing details on mintages, varieties, and values. It is suitable for collectors looking to manage and expand their Canadian coin collections.

Website: Canadian Coin https://canadiancoinnews.com/

Australian-Specific Applications

Australian Coin Collecting Blog
While primarily a blog, this site offers a wealth of information and a mobile-friendly interface for Australian coin collectors, including updates on new releases and historical data.

Website: Australian Coin Collecting Blog https://www.australiancoincollectingblog.com/

eCAC (eCollector Australian Coins)

eCAC is a specialized app for Australian coin collectors, providing information on coin values, mintages, and a platform for collectors to track and manage their collections.

Website: eCAC https://ecollector.com.au/

These apps and websites offer valuable resources for coin collectors in the USA, UK, Canada, and Australia, helping both novice and experienced collectors navigate the numismatic market effectively.

Top Coin Magazines

These knowledge resources are ideal for expanding your knowledge and not being caught off guard by the world of numismatics. Get to know everything they have to offer:

American Coin Magazines

COINage Magazine
Each monthly issue is filled with stories on current events and historical pieces on people, places, and events associated with coinage. They also feature information from leading numismatic authorities, beautiful color illustrations, and an up-to-date price guide.

To have all this information near you, just download the free app. Another feature within the app is that users can purchase the current publication and back issues.

Subscriptions are also available within the app. A subscription will start from the last regular issue at the time of your first purchase. A subscription to this magazine will automatically renew unless you cancel more than 24 hours before the end of the current period. You will be charged for renewal within 24 hours after the end of the current period, for the same duration and at the current subscription rate for the product.

Payment will be charged to your iTunes account at the time of purchase confirmation.

Users can register or log in to a Pocketmags account in the app. This will protect your data in the event of a lost device and allow you to search for purchases across multiple platforms. Existing Pocketmags users can retrieve their purchases by logging into their accounts.

You should load the app for the first time in a wifi area so that all app data is retrieved.

If your app does not load beyond the home page after a first installation or update, remove and reinstall from the App Store.

CoinWorld
This is one of the world's most popular non-academic publications for coin collectors, and it covers the entire numismatics field, including coins, paper money, medals, and tokens.

Coin World was founded as a weekly publication in 1960 by J. Oliver Amos, a seasoned editorial professional from the third generation of newspaper publishers. Amos brought his experience in the production of The Sidney Daily News to the coin field, applying what he learned from printing Linn's Stamp News.

In 1960, the concept of weekly coin publishing was new. At Coin World's 25th anniversary in 1985, Amos recounted that he saw "all the opportunities that could develop from a weekly presentation: club meetings around the country, personalities, and many other ideas we had learned from publishing The Sidney Daily News as a community newspaper."

Coin News
This is an information portal of daily coin news, articles, and updates on coins and collecting with free resources for collectors, such as coin price guides. Many can use the information to contrast with other sources.

Error Mint
This publication offers the latest news and information on collector's mint errors. There are over 1300 articles, features, findings, news, and information related to mint errors from the United States and around the world. The Mint Error News website has become the most popular and informative online resource on mint errors and is read by thousands of dealers and collectors.

UK, Canadian, Australian Coin Magazines

Coin News (UK)
Coin News is the leading publication for collectors of coins, medals, and banknotes in the UK. It provides news, features, and detailed information on British and world coins, helping collectors stay informed about the latest trends and market values.

Canadian Coin News
Canadian Coin News is a bi-weekly publication offering comprehensive coverage of the Canadian numismatic market. It includes articles on coin collecting, market trends, and historical pieces, as well as price guides and auction results.

Australasian Coin & Banknote Magazine
Australasian Coin & Banknote Magazine is the premier publication for collectors in Australia and New Zealand. It features news, market trends, detailed articles on coins and banknotes, and information on upcoming auctions and events.

These magazines and publications offer a wealth of information and resources for coin collectors across the USA, UK, Canada, and Australia, helping them stay informed and make educated decisions in the numismatic market.

Where to Find Investment Coins?

Here is a list of places where you can find investment coins, including specialized sites for the USA, Canada, UK, and Australia:

USA

Silver Gold Bull
It is one of those portals that offer a variety of services, among them the purchase and sale of investment coins at the same time. You just have to enter its page, as the name indicates, and check all the offers it has.

eBay
From new to used coins, you can find them in this online store, which undoubtedly offers a variety of options. It is advisable to enter and review their catalogs.

Yelp
More than a place, nowadays, you have many tools to find a pawn store in your state. One of the most popular options on the Internet is Yelp. You can use this service either from your

computer or from the application. This tool will help you locate a Pawn Shop based on your zip code, address, and city.

Numismatic Houses in Your State

Wherever you are in the United States, they may have a numismatic store nearby. Just use the application mentioned above and start your search for a coin store.

Gold and Silver Stores

It is common to find that investment piece in these stores if you have one nearby. These sites regularly have certification and specialized staff and are presented as a safe way to acquire a coin of this type.

Canada

Colonial Acres Coins

Offers a wide range of Canadian coins and numismatic supplies, with regular auctions and online shopping.

Silver Gold Bull Canada

The Canadian branch of Silver Gold Bull provides a similar range of services, including the purchase and sale of investment coins.

Gatewest Coin Ltd.

Specializes in Canadian coins and offers a comprehensive selection of numismatic items.

Canadian Coin & Currency

A leading dealer in Canadian coins, offering a vast selection of rare and collectible coins.

Coins Unlimited

Serving collectors with a wide selection of Canadian coins and numismatic supplies, as well as regular auctions.

UK

The Royal Mint

The official source for British coin information and current releases.

London Coin Auctions

Offers auctions specializing in British coins with online catalogs.

Spink & Son

One of the oldest and most respected coin dealers in the UK, offering a wide range of British and world coins.

Chards

A reputable dealer specializing in gold and silver coins, with a focus on investment-grade coins.

Coincraft

Located in London, this store offers a vast selection of British coins and provides expert advice.

Australia

The Perth Mint

The official source for Australian coin information and current releases.

Downies

A major dealer in Australian coins, offering a wide range of numismatic products and online auctions.

Royal Australian Mint

The official mint of Australia, providing information on current and historical coin releases.

Australian Coin Collecting Blog

A resource for Australian coin collectors, providing news and updates on new releases and historical data.

Coinworks

Specializing in rare and historical Australian coins, offering a selection of high-quality numismatic items.

These specialized sites provide comprehensive resources for coin collectors and investors in the USA, Canada, UK, and Australia, offering valuable information, market prices, and avenues for buying and selling coins.

STEP IV:

PROTECT YOUR INVESTMENT: HOW TO PROPERLY STORE AND DISPLAY YOUR COINS FOR MAXIMUM VALUE

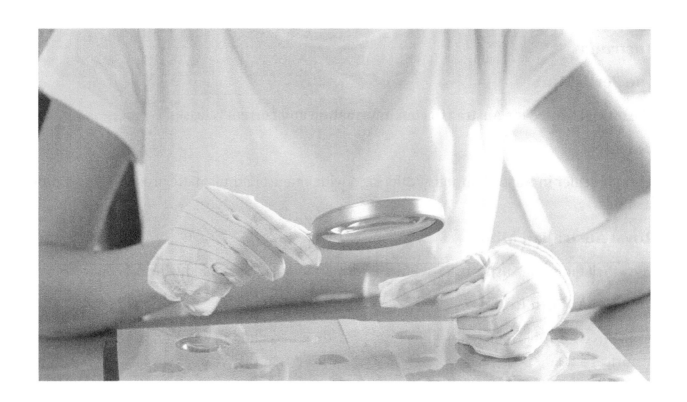

Chapter 6: How to Catalog a Coin Collection

Once you have reached this chapter, you may be thinking about those coins you have in your collection and wondering about their value. If you can't identify this detail, here you will learn how to do it and find out the value of what you own.

Find Out if Your Coin Collection That Has Been Locked in the Drawer for Years Has Some Value

Without a doubt, the first step is to know the value of the pieces that you inherited or have been collecting for some time. It is, therefore, important that you start by informing yourself.

In the previous chapters, there is enough information that will allow you to have a criterion on how to evaluate the value of a coin.

Another option is to visit the sites that numismatists frequent, such as the United States Mint, and obtain the official catalogs and manuals for selling coins.

This kind of knowledge will truly allow you to estimate the total value of your collection; knowledge is power.

But finally, keep in mind that if you are going to sell your coins to a numismatic house, auction house, or antique shop, all of these establishments need to make a profit; therefore, they will not buy your coins at the final price.

Seek Advice

When all options are exhausted and you wish to have a more reliable source, it is pertinent to consult with collectors. Also, do not fail to review the magazines named previously in this book, as you will find in them good information that will allow you to learn more about the value characteristics of a coin collection.

Another valuable step is to join numismatic societies or online forums where experienced collectors gather. These communities can provide insights and personal experiences that are invaluable. Don't hesitate to ask questions or seek opinions about specific coins in your collection. Additionally, attending coin shows and visiting local coin shops can offer opportunities to get professional appraisals and advice.

How and Why to Catalog a Coin Collection: Methods and Approaches

Using a catalog not only allows you to preserve your coins but also helps you classify the details of each coin.

Certainly, the process of cataloging does not mean simply putting coins together in an index or making an exhaustive notation of everything from the state of preservation and other properties of each coin.

The best thing is that this can be done within the catalog itself that includes these fields or in an Excel spreadsheet. These are individual cards, which are undoubtedly an excellent way to organize and account for what you have.

How to Organize a Coin Collection

Once you have all the necessary material, you should proceed with the classification since this will allow you to make all the relevant checks and the respective annotations. When it comes to classifying the coins, you should choose the form that best suits your collection. For example, if your collection is of a single country, you could classify them first by face value and second by year of issue or mintage.

In the case that your coins collection is from different countries, you could use the same classification, but first add data such as the different countries, as follows:

- Classification by country

- Classification by face value

- Sorting by year of issue (mintage)

Consider adding additional fields to your catalog for:

- *Condition/Grade*: Use standard grading terms like Good (G), Very Good (VG), Fine (F), Very Fine (VF), Extremely Fine (XF), and Mint State (MS).
- *Purchase Details*: Record where and when you acquired each coin, and for how much.
- *Historical Notes*: Include any interesting historical information or anecdotes related to the coin.

Insert Your Coins in Albums

This is undoubtedly the most orderly option and the most commonly used by those who are new to numismatics. The good point is that you can make the albums yourself or find them on the market.

Ensure that the albums or storage options you choose are made from materials that do not harm the coins. PVC-free plastic pages or Mylar flips are recommended for long-term storage as they prevent chemical reactions that can damage the coins. Label each section clearly and update your catalog regularly as you acquire or sell coins.

Cataloging and organizing your coin collection is not just about knowing what you have; it's about preserving the history and value of your collection. By following these steps, you'll ensure that your collection remains in top condition and that its value is accurately documented. This diligence will pay off whether you decide to sell your collection or pass it on to future generations.

Chapter 7: Clean and Store Collectible Coins Like an Expert

In this chapter, you will find a series of methods and expert advice on proper cleaning and storing coins stored in a drawer, preserving their value over time. Remember that they are pieces that require maintenance, and therefore it is important to know all the ways to do it to prevent them from deteriorating or suffering the consequences of remaining in storage.

The Main Causes of Damage to a Coin Collection

Before addressing the point of maintenance, you must know the factors that affect the condition of a piece, such as a coin.

I begin with the first and biggest enemy of a coin, which is humidity. Being copper and silver coins (the most common metals used in coin production), unfortunately, moisture is one of the main enemies of your pieces, as these two metals react chemically when they come in contact with water.

It is well known that water vapor is present in almost all environments, to varying degrees, and can seep into almost any object. It is certainly one of the most difficult environmental causes to prevent.

Heat, by itself, cannot damage coins. However, heat reduces the time it takes for a piece to be damaged by other environmental factors such as moisture, acids, and air pollution.

Another harmful element is cold, which can also spoil the delicate surface of uncirculated coins when moisture condenses into liquid water that is deposited on the coin's surface.

Acids are another deadly enemy of coins. That is why you should know that the most common source of acids, another deadly enemy of the coin, is found in collectible supplies made of standard paper and cardboard, where acid was used in the manufacturing process.

Although each metal or alloy presents its condition, which will depend on its composition and other factors, they all have in common the same type of care to avoid irreparable damage.

We assume that numismatic materials have undergone metallurgical processes that have transformed them into other products different from the mineral from which they came, which is the most stable form in which they were found in nature. All metals will try to regain stability with the environment, returning to their mineral form.

For this reason, over time, metallic objects become opaque, deteriorate and undergo oxidation and corrosion processes, acquiring an undesirable appearance that, in the numismatic sphere, makes them lose value.

Handling is one of the ways in which coins deteriorate and is due to improper treatment and/or carelessness. It is important to note that the skin secretes fatty acids that can be transferred to the metal surface through perspiration. This fact, together with the humidity of the environment and the oxygen in the air, can be the beginning of corrosion reactions.

How to Preserve Your Collectible Coins

It is crucial to always handle metal objects with clean gloves, preferably cotton or nitrile gloves underneath and cotton on top. The important idea is that they act as a barrier to prevent this transfer.

In case you do not know, coins and medals also have a way of being held; you should hold them by their edges to prevent scratches or incisions on their surface or force unnecessary twisting or pressure that can lead to cracks and breakage (in coins that are thin, fragile or very worn).

Handling should be done with the aid of a support, tray, or storage box. It is essential to control the environment by maintaining relatively low and stable humidity since such element contributes to the oxidation and corrosion of metals.

This objective can be difficult to achieve due to the climatic variables existing in some areas, and therefore it will depend, to a great extent, on the solutions that we give at home.

There are, however, two simple ways to maintain a low relative humidity:

- With the installation of dehumidifiers.

- Using humidity buffer materials.

In both cases, these are tools and materials that you can easily find on the market and that prevent excessive humidity, balancing it.

Another option is silica gel. You can find it packaged in the sachets that manufacturers usually put in the packaging boxes of products such as bags or shoes. They can also be found in specialized stores.

How to Clean Collectible Coins: 15 Expert Secrets for Cleaning and Storing Coins Stored in a Drawer

1. Avoid handling numismatic pieces directly with your hands; it is recommended to use thread or surgical gloves for handling and hold them by the edge.

2. It is not advisable to "clean" or polish the metal pieces with abrasives or solvents that, in the long run, cause greater damage to them.

3. Wash the coins lightly with soapy water (without polishing), rinse them, and give them a light acetone bath to dry them completely. This procedure can generally be used with all metals except for copper, which may suffer some oxidation.

4. For the storage of numismatic pieces, it is recommended to use inert paper and plastic, free of acidity; at the moment, a great variety of products of this type exist in the market.

5. In the case of metallic pieces with mirror or proof finish, they should never be removed from their capsules since they stain very easily when in contact with the hands.

6. Keep your collection away from liquids or substances that may accidentally damage it.

7. Avoid humid environments and direct exposure to sunlight.

8. Avoid at all costs any blow that could fracture the packaging.

9. You can place the coins in a study or bedroom away from the kitchen; this is the best option since oils and humidity can easily impregnate coin containers, folders, and albums.

10. Prepare a warm soapy water solution to clean them.

11. Use a soft bristle toothbrush with a solution to gently clean both sides of the coin.

12. When handling a coin, avoid using a damp cloth; instead, always use a clean, dry cloth (without rubbing).

13. To clean silver coins, one alternative is to soak them in natural lemon juice for five minutes.

14. For storage, make sure they are properly housed in a container, album, or folder specially designed for coins.

15. You can use acrylic trays or drawers but don't forget to keep them away from places where humidity will consume them.

There are different ways to store your coins in drawers, and they are as follows:

Container or Folder

Using a container or binder to store coins is reliable. In addition to protecting your coins from physical damage, coin folders help you organize your collection by giving you everything you need to place your coins, a method similar to an album. You can label them by dates, mintmarks, and additional information so that your coin collection is simultaneously cataloged and protected.

Metal Cabinet

Although not as secure as a safe deposit box, a metal cabinet will provide a safe environment for your collection because it does not have the problems associated with wood, i.e., the emission of organic chemicals that react negatively with metal compounds. Place the cabinet in a dry space or use a dehumidifier to reduce ambient humidity because metal tends to attract it in the form of condensation.

Bank Safe

Considering the idea of renting space in a bank safe deposit box for your coins is a good idea. Certainly, this is one of the safest places to store your coin collection.

This is possibly the most expensive solution, as bank vaults are built to keep criminals away from valuables, which is why they have the latest technology to provide security.

However, it is important to consider that the vaults are made of a material that will emit water vapor in case of fire, thus keeping the temperature inside the vault low.

Water vapor might be released into the vault over time, but the moisture can be absorbed by placing a silica gel pack inside the vault. This should be changed a couple of times a year to keep the gel fresh so that it can absorb as much moisture as possible.

Installing a Home or Office Safe

A less expensive option is to purchase a safe for your home or office to store your coin collection. Once you purchase the safe, there is no annual recurring fee like there is with a bank safe deposit box.

Home or office safes and bank vaults are made of the same material, so you should use a silica gel pack to absorb moisture and prevent coin damage.

How to Select the Right Chemicals to Restore Coins

Before taking this step, you must know your coin material because the element you use for a nickel coin can damage a silver coin, and so on. Remember that these pieces are also the product of alloys and may well have some kind of reaction to a detergent or cleaning chemical.

You can clean your collector or investment coins with neutral soap, ensuring they have a neutral ph. Use lukewarm distilled water: avoid hot water because it could damage the coin, while cold water will not clean enough. Let them soak for approximately half an hour. Dry with a soft towel, and always avoid absorbent cotton so that no residue remains.

Vinegar is another option, but first, put the coins under cold tap water pressure and then put the coins in a basin with warm water and 50% white vinegar. Let them stand for half an hour. This trick is especially effective for rust stains. Then dry them with a microfiber cloth.

You can also use salt and alcohol mixed in a container in the following proportions: three tablespoons of salt and a glass and a half of alcohol. Let the coins soak until you see that the dirt has come off; this process can take several days, so be patient.

Another option is to prepare a mixture of baking soda and lemon juice. Let the coins soak for a few minutes. When you take them out, you can clean them very carefully with a soft brush.

Another liquid that many do not know has cleaning functions is olive oil, as it is very effective when it comes to treating copper and bronze coins. Then, all you have to do is let them dry. If done carefully, the coins should not be damaged.

Use a soft eraser; it can be an ally as some stains may remain after cleaning.

How to Protect Collectible Coins

Before deciding where to store the coins, it is important to take into account aspects such as: keeping them out of the reach of children since they cannot understand their value or the importance of storing them so carefully.

Choose a place where they are kept dry, and for their proper conservation and to avoid problems such as rust, it is advisable not to keep them in damp areas of the house, such as near the kitchen or in a basement.

Use suitable materials to store them. There are many possibilities on the common market when it comes to choosing a container to keep coins, but you must select a receptacle made of a material specifically designed for this purpose.

To prevent any risk of loss due to fire or theft, you must think of safe places with temperature and humidity control to keep all your collections.

STEP V:

DON'T GET SCAMMED! LEARN THE SECRETS TO DETECTING COUNTERFEIT COINS TODAY!

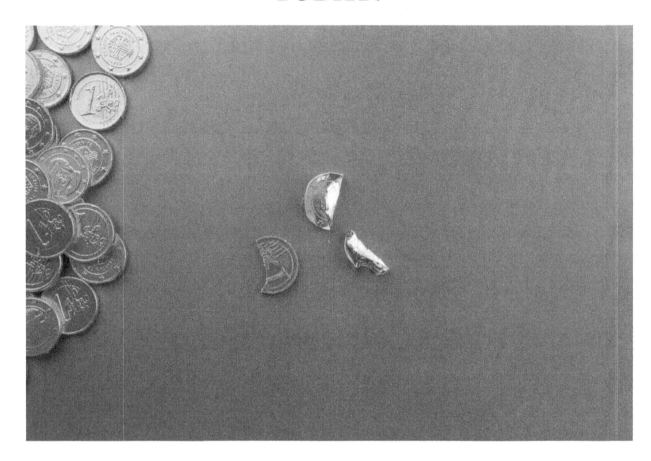

Chapter 8: Tools to Detect Fake or Counterfeit Coins as an Expert

In this chapter, you will see some accessories and tools that coin collectors use to check the pieces. However, the most important implement is you and your knowledge to do it in a simple and effective way.

How to Detect Counterfeit Coins

The good news is that counterfeit coins, due to their lower value, are not as prevalent, even when it comes to investment coins; counterfeiters find it more profitable to deal with banknotes.

Even so, the most affected currency in the case of Europe is the 2 euro, and its use is widespread in slot machines, tobacco machines, or vending machines. Sometimes they fail in terms of automatic reading and the identification of their electromagnetic characteristics.

All coins have a national side, indicating the issuing country, and a cross with a design. This design can be a map or a globe on which facts are shown or depicted.

To identify a counterfeit coin, look for the following:

Note: Don't forget to use the list of resources and information that have been explained throughout the book to make evaluations of the coins you are going to buy.

1. Start with a tactile examination where you should identify several details that have been mentioned throughout the book, from their physical appearance to the smallest details that catch your attention.

2. Try to identify the assembly: In bimetallic coins, the assembly of the perimetric ring is practically perfect so that, to the touch, no edge can be perceived at its junction with the core or center of the coin.

3. Another detail that can reveal if a coin is fake is the edge. This can be smooth, striated (series of parallel grooves in the thickness or edge of the coin), discontinuous striated (combination of parallel grooves and smooth parts), or with a perimeter groove. If there are burrs or other irregularities, it may be a counterfeit coin. You can usually find this information about a coin in the catalogs. Keep this in mind when examining the coin.

4. The texture of a coin is also key. Get to know it and determine if your piece has a smooth texture. If it feels slippery or soapy, it could be a melted coin and, therefore, counterfeit.

5. The color of a coin is characteristic and unique. That is why your knowledge is more essential than any tool. This color is because, in the manufacture of the coin, two or more metals are joined by casting (a process known as alloying).

6. The color is fixed when the metals are melted and remains unchanged throughout the coin's life. A particular case can be observed in Mexican coins that do not have any type of coating, nor do they have metallic plating or paint on them; therefore, they do not discolor.

7. The luster of a coin is obtained during minting and, like the color, is characteristic of each alloy. Reference is made to this detail in the previous chapters.

8. Smoothness can be identified and felt in the parts of the coin that are not engraved. They should be smooth, uniform, and without porosity. Believe it or not, a small detail like this can tell you a lot.

9. On the other hand, details like the wear of the coin are inevitable because when they are used daily, they suffer natural and irregular (uneven) wear. If a coin has regular or homogeneous (even) wear or has a general lack of sharpness in the engraving, then it may be a counterfeit coin.

10. Going into a deeper field, there is the "Latent Image." This is a characteristic that allows a change of image to be observed when the coin is moved to view it from different angles.

11. The micro text refers to text of very small size, requiring a magnifying glass to read it, one of the fundamental tools of a collector.

12. Comparative examination. After making an exhaustive review of the piece, it is important to carry out what is called the comparative examination.

13. In the case of doubting the authenticity of a coin, another determining factor is the weight; just by weighing it, you can determine if it is a counterfeit. It never hurts to use this device that can give you the exact measurements of the pieces.

14. Another detail that can tell you the presence of a counterfeit coin is the diameter and thickness. Remember that these characteristics are registered in a catalog of the Mint of the country that issued it, and these specifications are exact. Any difference in weight, diameter, or thickness may indicate that it is a counterfeit coin.

15. If your stored coin reacts to a liquid which it should not, it may also be a counterfeit. Immediately perform a thorough visual examination and then proceed to find an expert.

16. The origin of your purchase is very important because it may be a gift, and you do not know where it came from: whether it was bought in a store, from a numismatist, or anyone else.

What You Need to Know About a Coin to Learn How to Identify It

Obverse: Main side of the coin. It usually shows the issuer (name or bust of a hero or the Republic...).

Reverse: Opposite side of the obverse.

Type: It is the basic mint detail that shows the coin, the same in a more or less long issue.

Legend: The inscription shown on the coin is almost always circular around the central motif.

Value: The face value is the denomination. 1 dollar, 5 cents, etc.

Assayer: This is the acronym of the person in charge of the mint who controls the weight and grade of the coin. He is the guarantor of the gold or silver content and its weight according to the regulation of the issue.

Mint: The place where the coin is minted.

Weight: The coin is issued under competent authority. The weight of the coin is specified in the regulation where the issuance is established. Let us not forget that this is an essential element since the currency must respect more or less its intrinsic value.

That is why people took it and could give it because taking the minted gold or silver as a valuable item generated confidence. In other words, the coin weight is an important, essential characteristic. It may happen exceptionally that there is a strong (excessive) or weak (scarce) weight, but the error must be slight because the issue is regulated and had to pass certain quality control.

Original Luster

The intrinsic quality of the metal presents a shine, a natural reflection derived from the minting. This comes from the effect of the very strong blow to the metal with the dies, and the shine has not been lost by excessive circulation. It is a luster that comes from inside the metal, not the luster that surrounds the coin, and seems to plasticize it when it is clean, either by rubbing or other techniques. The original luster is the glow of the coined metal.

The shine from cleaning is like that of the chrome details on a bar counter; it is external to the metal and does not come from the inside. For banknotes, the original expression sizing is often used to specify the condition of the paper and ink, intaglio, and typography, the luster that maintains the banknote as freshly printed, or the remnants of that quality.

Conservation

It is an essential element for the value of the currency. Although it is an objective element, its perception and determination are sometimes subtle, complex, and very subjective. This division is commonly used:

Uncirculated (UC): Coin that fully preserves the original mintage qualities as it has not suffered any wear because it has not circulated. There may be some minor erosions or tiny insignificant taps produced by the contact between the different coins when they are handled in the bags or even by the effect of falling from the machine to the basket, but there is no wear even in the highest parts of the minted relief.

Extraordinarily Well Preserved (EBC): Coin that maintains a stupendous state of preservation even though it shows some minimal wear due to slight circulation; that is to say, only small wear in the most extreme part of the mint (the area that has regrown the most since it is the first to be lost) should be appreciated, but not beyond that point. Its presence must be very attractive, being the normal thing to preserve the original luster, even if they were remains.

Very Well Preserved (MBC): A coin that is in very acceptable condition for a circulated coin. It suffers general and uniform wear in the type of luster, although it may still have minimal traces of its original glow.

Well Preserved (WP): Coin that has circulated abundantly but maintains clearly identifiable essential data (issuer, value, date, mint, and assayer), and there is no doubt as to the type.

Regularly Circulated (RC): Highly circulated coins with certain deficiencies concerning the visibility or appreciation of the essential data, although the type can be identified.

Poorly Preserved (PP): Highly circulated and very worn coin, which has lost essential data and may even present difficulties in identifying the type.

The 15 Signs/Tips to Help You Prevent Fraud

1. Usually, scammers pose as well-known organizations. Scammers often pretend to communicate with you on behalf of a numismatic identity.

   They may use a real name or make up a name that looks official.

   Some may pose as a representative of a business you know, such as a precious metals dealer from a well-known store.

2. Generally, when they call to offer you a part, without first having contact with the person, be careful! Scammers have the technology to change the phone number that appears on your caller ID, so the name and number you see could be fake.

3. They may call you to offer you a part, as well as to buy (steal) from you.

4. Scammers put pressure on the person to act immediately. Remember, they want you to act before you take time to think about it. When they operate over the phone, they may tell you not to hang up so you can't verify their stories.

5. Some scammers try to intimidate you by threatening you, don't fall for this tactic. That is why it is important to be careful who you talk to about your collection; if you

go to a store or share in numismatic groups and one way or another, they find out what you have.

6. When you go to make a purchase, remember that the scammers tell you to pay in a specific way; this should be very careful. Don't fall for their methods right off the bat because of the temptation to buy or sell a piece.

   They usually insist that you pay by sending money through a money transfer company or by putting money on a gift card and giving them the number on the back. Others may send you a check (which will later turn out to be counterfeit) and tell you to deposit it and then send them money back.

7. This point relates to the previous one, and that is not to give out your personal or financial information in response to an unexpected request. Legitimate organizations that sell or buy coins will not call you or send you an email or text message asking for personal information, such as the number of your Social Security, bank account, or credit card.

8. Among the tips for detecting fraud, it is always advisable when in doubt to seek the testimonials of other people who have made purchases in this way. Those who experience or suspect they have witnessed fraud may have more criteria to tell you to do business or not, or simply give you ideas on how you can proceed more safely.

9. Your observation will always be key, and I am emphatic in all aspects when it comes to acquiring a collectible coin. Observation is a way to notice and identify if there is something that does not match and put you on alert. People who commit fraud usually exhibit some type of behavior that is quite unusual or strange, which, if carefully observed, can be a pretty accurate index of fraud.

10. Seek out other customers or suppliers and ask questions about the person who is offering you a product; you may get valuable and decisive information to make a decision.

11. Normally, scammers attract attention with special offers and persuade with false recommendations of supposed customers of coins in special sales and at special prices; do not fall for this trick to acquire a cheaper piece.

    The idea of these people is to persuade with special offers of reduced prices and then convince you to buy their items based on false recommendations.

12. Phantom product scams are just a part of internet fraud and online shoppers, but it is advisable to avoid paying through bank transfer, and if it is done, investigate well before who the buyer is or what you are buying.

13. Confirm authenticity: for collectibles, such as sports memorabilia, follow the steps required to confirm that the items are authentic.

14. Watch for warning signs: Is there a delay in shipping? Did you receive an unsolicited offer? Are they offering prices that are too low? Large quantities that are hard to find?

15. Finally, always use your common sense. If something doesn't add up, there's probably something wrong.

How to Create a List of Things to Follow and Look For

It is necessary in the case of someone starting to collect, and even more so if you are training your child, to let him know there are a series of steps to follow and what better than to create a list of things.

Basic Tools for a Coin Collector

To make your initial numismatic kit functional, you don't need a lot of specialized items as a collector, but a few key tools can help you appreciate and protect your coins.

Here are the must-haves to complete your toolkit:

- Magnifying glasses: Coins are small and can be extremely detailed: a magnifying glass with at least 7x magnification will reveal all the intricacies of your favorite designs.
- A way to store: Coins can be damaged by light, extreme temperatures, humidity, and even air. There are many ways to store coins safely; whatever you choose, be sure to use a product designed specifically for coins.
- Cotton gloves: Oil and dirt on your hands can damage coins, so try your best to avoid touching them. That said, sometimes you will need to handle them, so cotton gloves are a must. Use them only for your coins, and keep them clean and dry when not in use.
  Avoid using latex gloves; sometimes, they come with products that can cause damage to the coins.
- A reference source: You will probably want to learn more about the coins in your collection, the coins you would like to add to your collection, and coin collecting in

general. A good reference book or a reputable website will keep you informed and deepen your knowledge.

- A balance: This tool can be very useful to you, as one of the salient features of the coins in the catalog is the exact weight.

The Perfect Coin Collector's Checklist

Today, several companies have dedicated themselves to creating software designed to help coin collectors compile their lists. That's why we're telling you about programs, excellent tools for verifying the pieces you have in hand:

WorldCoins

This program, released in 2007 by ArteCode Software, combincs thc ability to inventory and organize coins in a single program. The program allows you to add an unlimited number of coins and descriptive information and up to four photos for each coin. It also has a search function to help you find information about some of the coins in your collection. The company's software only works on Microsoft Windows computers.

CoinManage

It was released in July 2009 and had a pre-installed database of more than 18,900 coins from the United States, Canada, and the United Kingdom. It also has information and images of 1,500 different coins to help with identification. Liberty Street Software, designed by CoinManage, touts the program's ability to produce real eBay auction results for various currencies.

Website---pyva.net/eng/chklist/---features

Website---pyva.net/eng/chklist/---features is a free program called checklist that works with smartphones and pocket PCs. You can download the program from the website.

Download Checklists

Some sites offer free, downloadable checklists for those who don't know. You can print out checklist sheets, fill in the blanks and submit your collection. One website--from *printablechecklists.com*--provides a printable PDF in standard 8-inch by 11-inch size.

It provides columns for coin year, mint marks, grade, price paid, value, and notes. Many coin dealer websites offer similar forms for collectors.

Catalog Help

This is a checklist that provides a great way to store data on your coin collection, but only some programs provide all the information you want to include in your list. Thus, the software programs include information on a limited number of coins. Therefore, collectors also need catalogs to do their check listings.

"The United States Coin Guide," known as the Red Book, provides a complete list of U.S. coins and retail coin prices. It is available in some bookstores and coin stores. In addition to printed catalogs, many websites provide coin price lists and other information. Some of them are Numismidea, PCGS, and ECoinprices, which provide online information on coin prices.

List of the Best Places in USA to Locate Coins

The following are excellent resources for finding collectible coins, whether for buying or selling:

1. **Newman Numismatic Portal**

An extensive archive of numismatic information, research, and auction results.

nnp.wustl.edu

2. **NGC World Price Guide**

Offers detailed price information for world coins, including British issues.

ngccoin.com/price-guide/world

3. **The United States Mint**

Official source for new U.S. coin releases and numismatic information.

catalog.usmint.gov

4. **PCGS Coin Facts**

Comprehensive information on coin grading, prices, and detailed photos.

pcgs.com/coinfacts

5. **Great Collections Inc**

A leading online coin auction house offering a wide selection of coins.

greatcollections.com

6. **Coin News**

Up-to-date news on coin markets and recent coin issues.

coinnews.net

7. PCGS

Professional Coin Grading Service, specializing in grading and certification.

pcgs.com

8. Mint Error News

Specializes in mint error coins and provides insights into errors and varieties.

minterrornews.com

Specialized UK, Canadian, Australian Coin Sites

UK

1. The Royal Mint

The official source for British coin information and current releases.

royalmint.com

2. Coin Yearbook

A reference guide with current UK coin values.

coinyearbook.co.uk

3. London Coin Auctions

Offers auctions specializing in British coins with online catalogs.

londoncoins.co.uk

4. Spink & Son

One of the oldest and most respected coin dealers in the UK, offering a wide range of British and world coins.

spink.com

CANADA

5. **Royal Canadian Mint**

Official source for new Canadian coin releases and numismatic information.

mint.ca

6. **Coins and Canada**

A comprehensive resource for Canadian coin prices, history, and news.

coinsandcanada.com

7. **Colonial Acres Coins**

Specializes in Canadian coins and offers a wide selection of collectible coins and accessories.

colonialacres.com

8. **Gatewest Coin Ltd.**

A reputable dealer offering Canadian coins, bullion, and collectibles.

gatewestcoin.com

AUSTRALIA

9. **The Perth Mint**

The official source for new Australian coin releases and precious metal products.

perthmint.com

10. **Royal Australian Mint**

Produces all of Australia's circulating coins and a range of collectible coins.

ramint.gov.au

11. **Downies**

A well-established dealer specializing in Australian coins and banknotes.

downies.com

12. **Australian Coin Collecting Blog**

Provides news, reviews, and insights on Australian coins.

australiancoincollectingblog.com

How to Pass on Your Coin Collection to Your Child

Who wouldn't like to have an inherited coin collection? The truth is many do, but this can rarely happen. Many people dedicate time and money to it and wish that the work is maintained and continues to grow.

Few people hope that their heirs will be the ones to continue with the collection and that it will keep on growing generation after generation. However, you can do it:

Try to tell your child in detail what your rounds are worth and how much he or she might get for them. But be realistic. Keep in mind also that, generally, a collection is worth in the hands of a collector considerably less than what that collector paid for the coins.

If you are doubtful that your collection will grow, try to discipline your child by providing clear instructions on what to do with the collection and how to increase it; perhaps this will encourage him or her to continue your legacy.

However, the ideal tip for your legacy to continue is to share it from this point on with your son or daughter. You can do this by employing strategies such as the following:

Telling stories of the pieces you own. I know that storytelling is not very appealing to children at first glance. However, you have the power to go all out and come up with interesting, fun stories that invite your child to learn more.

Children are naturally curious, and the intention is to awaken this quality in them, so I recommend that you use all your cards to your advantage. You can take a day of the week or month to take out your collection and reorganize it with your child.

You can also make it their homework to describe them and ask for their help in maintaining the pieces. The goal will always be to bring them closer and, above all, to show them the love you feel for them and the meaning of heritage and to leave them in charge of it.

This Is What Collecting Brings to Children

It is a healthy activity, which consists of the grouping and organization of objects of a certain category, which occupies people of all ages and in any geographical location.

Collecting is born as a personal interest, but the exchange, the search nurture it, and the readings related to the item being collected, and that is why it becomes the creation of constructive relationships with other people, inside or outside their environment and territory.

Collecting develops abilities of observation, constancy, perseverance, attention, details, classification methods, and others. These qualities make people improve themselves through the development of new and different skills that are characteristic of the best citizens, friends, students, professionals, workers, and even scientific researchers.

In the art of collecting, it is motivating and important to achieve the presentation of a given piece so that they cease to be lifeless entities and thus become pleasant companions of the time spent studying them.

Collecting, an Educational Activity for Young Children

If you want another perspective on collecting, we have the pedagogical point of view, where collecting is perceived as an educational activity that provides people with a series of tools through the search and acquisition of the pieces they are fascinated with.

Depending on the tastes and interests of each child, there are many options for starting a collection. This means that some children tend to be engaged with very educational subjects, such as collecting stones, minerals, fossils, etc., while others prefer more fun and playful things like comic book characters or soccer.

When collecting coins, it is important to learn more about the subject, its origin, its characteristics, or its properties. What starts as a hobby may end up becoming a passion or even a professional career. Although it may seem impossible, many children loved something so much as children that when they grew up, it helped them to carve out a professional path, for example, in the field of archeology or paleontology.

Chapter 9: 2025 COIN VALUE GUIDE | Discover the Most Valuable Coins and Their Current Market Prices

Here, for the collector, I present a list of interesting coins for collection. Remember that when collecting, the idea is to have special pieces that have set a precedent that you can obtain in the different places of sale and contribute to your hobby.

Some Americans might have nickels with very high values in their hands and simply not know it. Some British might have pounds with very high values in their hands and simply not know it. But thanks to new platforms where you can discover a lot of information from other collectors, it makes it easier for you to know what is in your hands.

Certainly, numismatics is taking over certain spaces, and you surely want to get into it, but you don't know where to start. That is why we give you some facts about the coins you can start with.

⇨ Check out the cool pics of the coins described in this chapter in the bonus on the next page

CLICK HERE TO DOWNLOAD IT

https://gdpublishing.aweb.page/p/5c2de7bd-8780-4c4c-afea-7444fcfe3d3a

OR SCAN QRCODE

Unlocking the Rich History of United States Coinage: Your Guide to Starting a Valuable Collection

The history of United States coinage is a fascinating journey that reflects the nation's growth and evolution. Beginning with the Coinage Act of 1792, which established the U.S. Mint and the first American coins, the progression of coinage in the United States has been marked by significant milestones and changes. From the early Draped Bust coins to the iconic Morgan and Peace dollars, each era brought its own unique designs and minting technologies.

Regular mint issues include a diverse array of denominations and designs, ranging from the penny to the dollar, each bearing unique features and historical significance. Understanding the role of different mints, such as those in Philadelphia, Denver, San Francisco, and West Point, along with their corresponding mint marks (P, D, S, W), is essential for any collector. These marks not only signify the origin of the coin but also add to its rarity and value, especially in cases of limited mintages.

Here is a list of United States coins with which you can start building your collection. All of them are available in the United States Coins catalog, so it would be good to start with them.

DOUBLE EAGLE (20$)

The Double Eagle is one of the most iconic coins in U.S. history, authorized by Congress on March 3, 1849. This $20 gold coin has two main designs: the Liberty Head and the Saint-Gaudens.

The **Liberty Head Double Eagle (1849-1907)** comes in two primary versions. The first is the "Without Motto" (1849-1866), where the reverse does not feature the motto "IN GOD WE TRUST." These coins are highly valued, especially the earlier dates, and can fetch prices ranging from $2,000 to over $10,000 depending on their condition and rarity. The second version is the "With Motto" (1866-1907), where the motto is placed above the eagle on the reverse. These are generally less rare than the without motto versions but still hold significant value, typically ranging from $1,500 to $8,000.

The **Saint-Gaudens Double Eagle (1907-1933)** is celebrated for its stunning design. The first version is the Ultra High Relief Pattern, MCMVII (1907), which is extremely rare and can be worth over a million dollars. Following this is the "Without Motto" (1907-1908) High Relief, MCMVII (1907), which features Arabic numerals and commands prices between $10,000 and $50,000. Later, from 1908 to 1933, the coins were issued with the motto "IN GOD WE TRUST," known as the "With Motto" version, which generally values between $1,500 and $5,000, though rarer dates can be worth significantly more.

→ **QUARTERMAN'S SELECTION OF COINS**

1908 St. Gaudens $20 Gold Coin Arabic Numerals No Motto

The Saint-Gaudens $20 gold coin was first minted by the United States Mint in 1907. The first coins were minted in an ultra-high break, but they were too complicated to strike correctly and did not heap carefully for bankers. In 1908, engravers at the mint reduced the relief, and the coins were ready for production. Many numismatists agreed that the Saint-Gaudens $20 gold coin is the most beautiful coin ever produced by the United States Mint.

To begin, the motto "IN GOD WE TRUST" was not included in Augustus Saint-Gaudens' unique design. At the end of 1908, the design was changed to include the motto behind the coin. The "No Motto" coin is reasonably priced given that it is a gold coin that will add value to a coin collection.

EAGLE (10$)

The Eagle coin, authorized by Congress on April 2, 1792, is a vital part of American numismatic history. This $10 gold coin has seen several design changes since its inception.

The **Capped Bust to Right (1795-1804)** includes two main versions. The "Small Eagle Reverse" (1795-1797) is highly sought after, with values typically starting at $20,000 for lower grades and reaching over $200,000 for high-grade specimens. The "Heraldic Eagle Reverse" (1797-1804) tends to be slightly less valuable but still commands high prices, usually ranging from $10,000 to $100,000 depending on condition and date.

The **Liberty Head (1838-1907)** series also has two varieties. The "No Motto Above Eagle" (1838-1866) is prized among collectors, with values ranging from $1,000 to $10,000, though some rare dates can exceed these ranges. The "Motto Above Eagle" (1866-1907) variety is more commonly found and typically valued between $700 and $5,000.

The **Indian Head (1907-1933)** Eagle features two varieties. The first, "No Motto on Reverse" (1907-1908), can be worth between $800 and $5,000. The second, "Motto on Reverse" (1908-1933), is slightly more common, with values generally ranging from $700 to $3,000. As with all coins, the exact value depends significantly on the coin's condition and rarity.

→ **QUARTERMAN'S SELECTION OF COINS**

Eagle $10 Gold Coin 1804 (NGC PR65, Deep Cameo)

In 1804 the United States Mint stopped producing $10 gold eagles, the largest denomination at the time. When Andrew Jackson wanted to provide unique sets featuring one instance of each U.S. currency denomination in use as gifts on diplomatic visits from 1834 to 1835, the Mint would have to blend the dies from the 'gold eagle' with the minting technology available in the 1830s. It is believed that six of these coins were made confirming that three have survived. The ANA has one on loan for its gallery, and the other two are controlled remotely. A specimen owned by legendary collector Colonel

E.H.R. Green and former Secretary "William Woodin" sold for $5 million at a private auction in 2007. Owner Bob R. Simpson sold another coin, an "NGC PR65 DC," for an unknown sum in 2020.

10 Dollars (Indian Head-Eagle) 1907 of the United States of America

The 10 dollars (Indian Head-Eagle) coin of 1907 belongs to the United States coin catalog. You can find this coin in users' collections and find out its numismatic value.

Features:

Features:

Name: 10 dollars (Indian Head-Eagle)

Shape: Round

Material: Gold (0,900)

Weight (g): 16.72 g

Diameter (mm): 27,00 mm

Edge: Fluted

Obverse: LIBERTY 1907

Reverse: UNITED STATES OF AMERICA E PLURIBUS UNUM TEN DOLLARS

Price: $871.65

HALF EAGLE (5$)

The Half Eagle, authorized by Congress and first minted in 1795, is a significant piece in U.S. coin history. This $5 gold coin has evolved through several design changes over the years.

The **Capped Bust to Right (1795-1807)** comes in two primary versions. The first is the "Small Eagle Reverse" (1795-1798), known for its delicate design and historical value, with prices ranging from $10,000 to $50,000 depending on the condition. The second is the "Heraldic Eagle Reverse" (1795-1807), which features a more robust eagle design and typically values between $5,000 and $30,000.

The **Draped Bust to Left (1807-1812)** coins are rare and highly prized by collectors. These coins generally range from $10,000 to $40,000, depending on their condition and specific year of minting.

The **Capped Head to Left (1813-1834)** has three subtypes. The "Bold Relief" (1813-1815) is highly valued, often ranging from $15,000 to $50,000. The "Large Diameter" (1813-1829) and the "Reduced Diameter" (1829-1834) varieties vary in value from $5,000 to $25,000 based on their state of preservation.

The **Classic Head, No Motto (1834-1838)** is a relatively short-lived series, generally valued between $2,000 and $10,000, with rarer dates commanding higher prices.

The **Liberty Head (1839-1908)** includes two varieties. The "No Motto Above Eagle" (1839-1866) tends to be more valuable, ranging from $1,000 to $7,000. The "Motto Above Eagle" (1866-1908) is more common but still valuable, with prices from $600 to $3,000.

The **Indian Head (1908-1929)** is known for its unique incuse design, making it a favorite among collectors. These coins typically range from $300 to $1,500, though certain years and conditions can exceed these values.

QUARTER EAGLE (2,50$)

The Quarter Eagle, authorized by Congress on April 2, 1792, is a smaller denomination gold coin that has seen various design changes throughout its history.

The **Capped Bust to Right (1796-1807)** is one of the earliest versions, known for its classic design. These coins are highly sought after, with values ranging from $10,000 to $50,000 based on condition.

The **Draped Bust to Left, Large Size (1808)** is a one-year type coin, making it particularly rare and valuable, typically fetching between $20,000 and $80,000.

The **Capped Head to Left (1821-1834)** includes the "Large Diameter" (1821-1827) and the "Reduced Diameter" (1829-1834) versions. Values for these coins generally range from $5,000 to $30,000, with condition playing a significant role in their worth.

The **Classic Head, No Motto on Reverse (1834-1839)** is valued between $1,500 and $10,000, depending on the year and condition.

The **Liberty Head (1840-1907)** includes the special **CAL. Gold Quarter Eagle (1848)**, struck from California gold. Regular Liberty Head coins range from $300 to $1,500, while the CAL. variety is highly coveted and can fetch upwards of $10,000 to $50,000.

The **Indian Head (1908-1929)** features a unique recessed design. These coins typically range in value from $300 to $2,000, with some years and conditions commanding higher prices.

DOLLAR (1$)

The U.S. dollar coin has a rich history, beginning with its authorization in 1792. Here is a detailed guide to its major versions and their values.

The **Flowing Hair (1794-1795)** is the first dollar coin issued by the U.S. Mint. It features a flowing-haired Liberty on the obverse and a small eagle on the reverse. These coins are highly collectible, with values ranging from $50,000 to over $1,000,000 depending on condition and provenance.

The **Draped Bust (1795-1804)** comes in two main types. The "Small Eagle Reverse" (1795-1798) is valued between $1,000 and $100,000, while the "Heraldic Eagle Reverse" (1798-1804) ranges from $2,000 to $200,000. The **1804 Dollar** is one of the most famous and rare U.S. coins, often fetching over $1,000,000 at auction.

The **Gobrecht Dollars (1836-1839)**, named after their designer Christian Gobrecht, are known for their beautiful designs and rarity. These coins typically range from $5,000 to $30,000.

The **Liberty Seated (1840-1873)** series includes two varieties. The "No Motto" (1840-1865) coins range from $300 to $3,000, while the "With Motto" (1866-1873) versions are valued between $400 and $5,000.

The **Trade Dollars (1873-1885)** were minted primarily for trade in Asia. They are highly collectible, with values typically ranging from $150 to $3,000.

The **Morgan Dollar (1878-1921)** is one of the most popular U.S. coins among collectors. Depending on the year and mintmark, these coins can range from $25 to $1,000 or more for key dates in high condition.

The **Peace Dollar (1921-1935)** commemorates the end of World War I. Values range from $30 to $300, with some rare dates exceeding these amounts.

The **Eisenhower Dollar (1971-1978)** features three main varieties: "Eagle Reverse" (1971-1974), "Bicentennial" (1776-1976), and "Eagle Reverse Resumed" (1977-1978). These coins typically range from $1.50 to $50.

The **Susan B. Anthony Dollar (1979-1999)** has a distinctive design and is valued between $1 and $10, with some proof versions fetching higher prices.

The **Sacagawea Dollar (2000-2008)** features the famous Native American guide and ranges from $1 to $10, depending on the year and mintmark.

The **Presidential Dollar (2007-2016, 2020)** series honors U.S. Presidents, with values typically ranging from $1 to $5.

The **Native American Dollar (2009 to date)** features a different reverse design each year, celebrating Native American contributions. Values generally range from $1 to $5.

The **American Innovation Dollar (2018 to date)** features a new design annually, celebrating American innovation. Values typically range from $1 to $5.

The **1921 Silver Dollar Anniversary Coins** were issued to commemorate the Morgan and Peace dollars, with values ranging from $50 to $200 depending on the specific issue.

The **Gold Dollar** has three main designs:

- **Liberty Head (1849-1854)**: Valued from $150 to $500.
- **Indian Princess Head, Small Head (1854-1856)**: Typically ranges from $200 to $600.
- **Indian Princess Head, Large Head (1856-1889)**: Values range from $200 to $700.

→ QUARTERMAN'S SELECTION OF COINS

Flowing Hair Dollar 1794 (PCGS SP66)

This piece, the best-known specimen of the 1st silver dollar made by the United States Mint, held the previous best record for the most expensive coin. It was acquired by Bruce Morelan in 2013 for $10,016,875 and auctioned last October after failing to meet its reserve price. The initial mintage was 1,758 coins; however, many have been melted due to low quality. Around 130 copies of this coin remaining were created as presents for VIPs.

At least for the moment, the 1794 Flowing Hair Silver Dollar might be considered the priciest coin ever sold. According to some scholars, it was the U.S. Mint's first silver dollar to be produced. The reverse has an American eagle, while the front depicts a portrait of Lady Liberty with flowing hair. Those coins were created in extremely small quantities — fewer than 1,800 were ever made — and one expert estimate that there are still 120 to 130 of them in existence. In 2013, the coin brought slightly over $10 million at auction.

This $1-denominated coin lacks a mint mark. It was sold in 2013 at the Stack's Bowers Galleries' auction house for $10 million.

According to experts, this was the first silver dollar struck by the U.S. mint and the finest coin of its era still extant. The 1974 Flowing Hair Dollar is historically significant because it was the first dollar coin to be standardized nationwide.

1921 Peace Dollar — High Relief

Anthony DeFrancisci made the Peace Silver Dollar, and at first, it was made in December 1921. The U.S. Mint also made an important mintage of 1921 dated the Morgan silver dollars. The notion of commemorating the peace following the "Great War" was first suggested by Farran Zerbe, ex-President of the American Numismatic Association, beginning from 1908 to 1910. The idea was successful, after which DeFrancisci made an attractive design symbolic of liberty at the front and peace indicated by an "American Eagle" at the back.

Although the Peace silver dollar coins were a great help but were too hard to strike through properly, the dies' breaks were so deep that the metal could not flow completely into these deep breaks and produced insufficient detail on the coins. The mint didn't just begin to strike these coins until December 26, 1921. This delayed start gave a wonderful inadequate time for the United States Mint to make these new dollars. To some extent, they could strike more than a million coins, and the community quickly took a picture of them. Though these coins are somehow rare, a collector just starting can get a distributed sample at a reasonable cost.

Dollars in Morgan Silver

The Morgan Silver Dollar is a massive dollar coin with the image of Lady Liberty on the obverse and an eagle on the reverse. It was named after its designer, engraver George T. Morgan. Its official minting began in 1878 and lasted until 1921. It's an ancient coin. The US government will issue this coin as a one-of-a-kind non-circulating currency in 2021. This coin was difficult to find prior to 2021.

This means that finding one of these coins will be easier starting in 2021, so you might want to take advantage of this. This currency was produced by four distinct mints, each with its own distinctive mark. Only Philadelphia does not have a symbol. I would not recommend seeking this coin if you collect coins for their history or design, but if you are looking for a profitable investment, this is probably the coin for you. The value of the Morgan Silver Dollar has risen dramatically over time and may rise even further.

Even though Morgan silver dollars aren't particularly rare in and of themselves, several of the older vintages can fetch exorbitant prices. If you don't have any of the more uncommon varieties, the Morgan is simply a stunning object with the substantial sensation of a balanced coin that is 90% silver.

Considering the silver content as well as the value of the unique metal, a "run-of-the-mint" Morgan should sell for at least $20. The accompanying Morgan examples, nevertheless, can sell for much more; just be sure to focus on the mint mark, which is an alphabetical designation on some coins:

- S. Morgan, 1893
- Morgan, 1901
- CC Morgan in 1889
- S. Morgan, 1884
- Morgan 1893

If in mint condition, all of these might fetch between $100,000 and $550,000, as per Coin Trackers. Additionally, there are additional Morgan silver dollars that can be purchased for thousands of dollars.

If you appreciate the way the Morgan silver dollar looks, it won't cost you much to purchase one of the more affordable examples, and you'll be able to own such a part of history without paying a large price.

The 2007 'Godless' Presidential Dollar Coin

Every US currency bears the infamous "In God We Trust" inscription, but not all of them did, at least not in 2007. The new George Washington one-dollar coins were released in the United States this year. It is said that an unknown number of them were not inscribed with the infamous 'logo' by mistake. They're known as "Godless" dollars here, but the official name is "Missing Edge Lettering" dollars. Tens of thousands of these coins have been discovered, with prices ranging from $29 to $228.

1 Dollar (Indian Head) 1856-1883 from the United States

The 1-dollar (Indian Head) coin of 1856-1883 belongs to the United States coin catalog.

Features:

Name: 1 dollar (Indian Head)

Shape: Round

Material: Gold (0,900)

Weight (g): 1,67 g

Diameter (mm): 15,00 mm

1 Dollar (Eisenhower Bicentennial Dollar) 1976-1-1976S2 of the United States of America

The 1-dollar (Eisenhower Bicentennial Dollar) coin of 1976-1-1976S2 belongs to the United States coin catalog.

Features:

Name: 1 dollar (Eisenhower Bicentennial Dollar)

Shape: Round

Material: Copper-nickel

Weight (g):22,68 g

Diameter (mm):38,10 mm

Edge: Fluted

Price: $2.25

1 Dollar (Susan B. Anthony Dollar) 1979D-1999P of the United States

The 1-dollar (Susan B. Anthony Dollar) coin of 1979D-1999P belongs to the United States coin catalog.

Features:

Name: 1 dollar (Susan B. Anthony Dollar)

Shape: Round

Material: Copper-Nickel

Weight (g):8,10 g

Diameter (mm):26,50 mm

Edge: Fluted

Price: 1,00€ - 600,00$.

1 Dollar (Herreshoff's Reliance Yacht - Rhode Island) 2022D-2022P of United States

The 1-dollar (Herreshoff's Reliance Yacht Reliance - Rhode Island) coin of 2022D-2022P belongs to the United States coin catalog.

Features:

Name: 1 dollar (Herreshoff's Yacht Reliance - Rhode Island)

Shape: Round

Material: Copper-nickel-zinc

Weight (g): 8,10 g

Diameter (mm): 26.49 mm

Edge: Plain with inscription 2022 D E PLURIBUS UNUM

Obverse: IN GOD WE TRUST

Reverse: UNITED STATES OF AMERICA RHODE ISLAND

Price: 1,80 dollar - 14,84 dollar

1 Dollar (Walking Liberty) 1986-2020 of the United States of America

The 1-dollar (Walking Liberty) coin of 1986-2020 belongs to the United States coin catalog.

Features:

Name: 1 dollar (Walking Liberty)

Shape: Round

Material: Silver (0,999)

Weight (g): 31,11 g

Diameter (mm): 40,60 mm

Edge: Plain

Price: 16,76€ - 61,00€.

1 Dollar (United States Capitol Bicentennial) 1994 of the United States of America

The 1-dollar (United States Capitol Bicentennial) 1994 coin belongs to the United States coin catalog.

Features:

Name: 1 dollar (United States Capitol Bicentennial)

Shape: Round

Material: Silver (0,900)

Weight (g):26,73 g

Diameter (mm): 38,10 mm

Edge: Fluted

Price: 35,24$.

1 Dollar (Centennial Olympic Games-Gymnastics) 1995 from the United States

The 1-dollar (Centennial Olympic Games-Gymnastics) coin of 1995 belongs to the United States coin catalog.

Features:

Name: 1 dollar (Centennial Olympic Games-Gymnastics)

Shape: Round

Material: Silver (0,900)

Weight (g): 26,73 g

Diameter (mm): 38,10 mm;

Price: $ 2.30

1 Dollar (Soccer World Cup USA) 1994 of the United States of America

The 1-dollar (USA Soccer World Championship) coin of 1994 belongs to the United States coin catalog.

Features:

Name: 1 dollar (USA Soccer World Championship)

Shape: Round

Material: Silver

Weight (g):26,73 g

Diameter (mm):38,10 mm

Edge: Fluted

Price: 22,08$

1 Dollar (V Centennial of the Voyage of Columbus) 1992 of the United States

The 1992 1-dollar (V Centennial of the Voyage of Columbus) coin belongs to the United States coin catalog.

Features:

Features:

Name: 1 dollar (V Centennial of the Voyage of Columbus)

Shape: Round

Material: Silver (0,900)

Weight (g): 26,73 g

Diameter (mm): 38,10 mm

Edge: Fluted

Price: 54,94€

1 Dollar (200th Anniversary of the White House) of the United States 1992

The 1-dollar (200th Anniversary of the White House) coin of 1992 belongs to the United States coin catalog. You can find this coin in users' collections and know its numismatic value.

The price ranges from $36.26 to $49.71, depending on the condition.

Features:

Name: 1 dollar (200th Anniversary of the White House).

Shape: Round

Material: Silver (0,900)

Weight (g):26,73 g

Diameter (mm):38,10 mm

Edge: Fluted

Price: 36,264 - 49,71$

1 Dollar (Sacagawea Dollar) 2000D-2008S of the United States

The 1-dollar (Sacagawea Dollar) coin of 2000D-2008S belongs to the United States coin catalog.

Features:

Name:1 dollar (Sacagawea Dollar)

Shape: Round

Material: Copper-zinc-manganese-nickel

Weight (g):8,07 g

Diameter (mm):26,50 mm

Edge: Smooth

Price: 1,00$ - 239,49$.

The Sacagawea dollar, also known as the "gold dollar," is a United States dollar coin that has been minted since 2000, although it was not released for general circulation between 2002 and 2008 and again in 2012 due to its general unpopularity among the population and low business demand for this piece.

These coins are characterized by a manganese-brass plated copper core, which gives them a distinctive golden color. The coin's obverse design is the work of Glenna Goodacre. Between 2000 and 2008, the reverse featured an eagle designed by Thomas D. Rogers. However, since 2009, it has changed each year, with each depicting a different aspect of Native American culture.

The coin was first suggested to replace the Susan B. Anthony dollar, which proved useful for vending machine operators and transportation systems despite being unpopular with the public. Originally, the Statue of Liberty was proposed as a model, but Sacagawea, the Shoshone that guided the Lewis and Clark expedition, was eventually chosen.

1 Dollar (US President - Thomas Jefferson) coin of 2007D-2007S

The 1-dollar (US President - Thomas Jefferson) coin of 2007D-2007S belongs to the United States coin catalog.

Features:

Name: 1 dollar (U.S. President - Thomas Jefferson)

Shape: Round

Material: Copper-zinc-manganese-nickel

Weight (g):8,07 g

Diameter (mm):26,50 mm

Edge: Plain with inscription *** E PLUBIRUS UNUM *** Year and mint.

Price: 0,85$ - 3,25$.

The 1 Dollar Commemorative Coin referring to 3rd President "Thomas Jefferson" is of UNC quality; the coin commemorates "Thomas Jefferson" randomly from the unique mark.

The coin is part of the series dedicated to the Presidents of the United States of America, depicting on the reverse the face of the 3rd President "Thomas Jefferson" and the Statue of Liberty on the obverse.

1 Dollar (Sacagawea Dollar - Native American Dollar - Wampanoag Treaty 1621) 2011D-2011S of the United States

The 1-dollar (Sacagawea Dollar - Native American Dollar - Wampanoag Treaty 1621) coin of 2011D-2011S belongs to the United States coin catalog.

Features:

Name: 1 dollar (Sacagawea Dollar - Native American Dollar - Wampanoag Treaty 1621)

Shape: Round

Material: Copper-zinc-manganese-nickel

Weight (g):8,07 g

Diameter (mm):26.50 mm

Edge: *** E PLUBIRUS UNUM *** Year and mint *** E PLUBIRUS UNUM *** Year and mint.

Price: 1,50$ - 135,00$

Knowing the key dates, rarities, and varieties of the Sacagawea dollar will teach you to recognize that minor differences in a coin can mean significant differences in its value. Therefore, it is advisable to study its descriptions and images to identify these valuable coins in the Sacagawea dollar.

Many factors go into determining the value of a coin, some of which are quite valuable and some of which are not. Therefore, it is recommended that you consult the Sacagawea value and price guide for current market trends for these coins.

If you are unsure whether you have one of these valuable coins, you can take it to a local coin dealer or coin expert to get their opinion. Remember, not all dealers are experts in all types of coins.

HALF DOLLAR (1/2 $)

The Half Dollar, one of the enduring denominations in U.S. coinage, has seen numerous design changes since its inception in 1794. Here's an overview of its main versions and their values.

Flowing Hair (1794-1795)

The **Flowing Hair Half Dollar (1794-1795)** is the earliest half dollar issued by the U.S. Mint. These coins feature a portrait of Liberty with flowing hair on the obverse and a small eagle on the reverse. Values for these coins can range from $10,000 to over $100,000 depending on their condition.

Draped Bust (1796-1807)

The **Draped Bust Half Dollar (1796-1807)** comes in two main versions. The "Small Eagle Reverse" (1796-1797) is rare and highly prized, often valued between $20,000 and $100,000. The "Heraldic Eagle Reverse" (1801-1807) is more common, with values ranging from $1,000 to $20,000.

Capped Bust, Lettered Edge (1807-1836)

The **Capped Bust, Lettered Edge Half Dollar (1807-1836)** also has two styles. The "First Style" (1807-1808) typically ranges from $200 to $2,000, while the "Remodeled Portrait and Eagle" (1809-1836) can be valued between $100 and $1,500, depending on condition and date.

Capped Bust, Reeded Edge (1836-1839)

The **Capped Bust, Reeded Edge Half Dollar (1836-1839)** features two reverse inscriptions. The "Reverse 50 CENTS" (1836-1837) can be valued from $500 to

$5,000. The "Reverse HALF DOL" (1838-1839) generally ranges from $300 to $3,000.

Liberty Seated (1839-1891)

The **Liberty Seated Half Dollar (1839-1891)** has several varieties:

- **Variety 1 - No Motto Above Eagle (1839-1853)**: Values range from $20 to $200.
- **Variety 2 - Arrows at Date, Rays Around Eagle (1853)**: Typically valued between $50 and $500.
- **Variety 3 - Arrows at Date, No Rays (1854-1855)**: Ranges from $30 to $300.
- **Variety 4 - Motto Above Eagle (1866-1873)**: Values range from $25 to $250.
- **Variety 5 - Arrows at Date (1873-1874)**: Ranges from $30 to $300.

Barber (1892-1915)

The **Barber Half Dollar (1892-1915)**, known for its classic design, is valued between $10 and $500, with higher prices for better conditions and rare dates.

Liberty Walking (1916-1947)

The **Liberty Walking Half Dollar (1916-1947)** is popular among collectors. Values range from $10 to $1,000 depending on the year and condition, with rare dates commanding higher prices.

Franklin (1948-1963)

The **Franklin Half Dollar (1948-1963)** features Benjamin Franklin and is generally valued between $10 and $50, though certain proof versions can be worth more.

Kennedy (1964 to Date)

The **Kennedy Half Dollar (1964 to date)** has several versions:

- **Silver Coinage (1964)**: Valued between $10 and $30.
- **Clad Coinage and Silver Proofs (1971 to date)**: Typically range from $1 to $10.
- **Bicentennial (1776-1976)**: Values range from $2 to $10.
- **Eagle Reverse Resumes (1977 to date)**: Generally valued at face value, though some proof versions can be higher.
- from $200 to $700.

→ QUARTERMAN'S SELECTION OF COINS

1/2 Dollar (50 cents) (Kennedy Half Dollar) 1971-1974S of the United States

The 1/2-dollar (50 cents) (Kennedy Half Dollar) coin of 1971-1974S belongs to the United States coin catalog.

Features:

Name: 1/2 dollar (50 cents) (Kennedy Half Dollar)

Shape: Round

Material: Copper-plated copper-nickel

Weight (g): 11,34 g

Diameter (mm): 30,60 mm

Edge: Reeded

Price: 0.50$ - 468.02$.

The 1971-D Kennedy Half was minted by the Denver Mint, while the rest were proofs struck at San Francisco Mint. The 1971-D Kennedy Half Dollar is in bright uncirculated condition and exhibits uninterrupted edge-to-edge luster. The Denver Mint produced over 305 million half dollars in 1971, lending at low premiums and easy access for the series.

John F. Kennedy is the famous president who was assassinated in November 1963. But Kennedy has a mark in history beyond his death. During his 2-year term, he constantly dealt with high tensions between communism and the United States. Kennedy remains the only Roman Catholic to have served as president of the United States.

1/2 Dollar (50 cents) (Kennedy Half Dollar, Bicentennial) of the United States 1976

The 1/2-dollar (50 cents) (Kennedy Half Dollar, Bicentennial) coin of 1976 belongs to the United States coin catalog.

Features:

Name: 1/2 dollar (50 cents) (Kennedy Half Dollar, Bicentennial)

Shape: Round

Material: Silver (0,400)

Weight (g): 11,50 g

Diameter (mm): 31,00 mm

Edge: Reeded

Price: 50,00$.

QUARTER DOLLAR (1/4 $)

The U.S. Quarter Dollar has a storied history, beginning in 1794. Here's a breakdown of its primary versions and their values.

Draped Bust (1796-1807)

The **Draped Bust Half Dollar (1796-1807)** features two main versions:

- **Small Eagle Reverse (1796)**: Known for its rarity, these coins can range in value from $20,000 to over $100,000 depending on condition.
- **Heraldic Eagle Reverse (1801-1807)**: Featuring a more robust eagle design, these coins are typically valued between $1,000 and $20,000.

Capped Bust (1815-1838)

The **Capped Bust Half Dollar (1815-1838)** has two varieties:

- **Large Diameter (1815-1828)**: Values range from $50 to $1,000, depending on condition and rarity.
- **Reduced Diameter (1831-1838)**, with the motto removed: These coins are generally valued between $40 and $800.

Liberty Seated (1838-1891)

The **Liberty Seated Half Dollar (1838-1891)** comes in several varieties:

- **Variety 1 - No Motto Above Eagle (1838-1853)**: Values range from $20 to $300.
- **Variety 2 - Arrows at Date, Rays Around Eagle (1853)**: Typically valued between $50 and $500.
- **Variety 3 - Arrows at Date, No Rays (1854-1855)**: Ranges from $30 to $300.
- **Variety 4 - Motto Above Eagle (1866-1873)**: Values range from $25 to $250.

- **Variety 5 - Arrows at Date (1873-1874)**: Ranges from $30 to $300.

Barber (1892-1916)

The **Barber Half Dollar (1892-1916)** is known for its classic design. These coins are valued between $10 and $500, with higher prices for better conditions and rare dates.

Standing Liberty (1916-1930)

The **Standing Liberty Half Dollar (1916-1930)** features two varieties:

- **Variety 1 - No Stars Below Eagle (1916-1917)**: Typically valued between $50 and $1,000.
- **Variety 2 - Stars Below Eagle (1917-1930)**: Values range from $25 to $500.

Washington (1932 to Date)

The **Washington Quarter (1932 to date)** has several key versions:

- **Silver Coinage (1932-1964)**: Typically valued between $5 and $50.
- **Clad Coinage and Silver Proofs (1965 to date)**: Generally valued at face value to $5, though proof coins can be higher.

- **Bicentennial (1776-1976)**: Values range from $1 to $10.
- **State Quarter (1999-2008)**: Generally valued at face value, with some proofs and special issues worth more.
- **American Women (2022-2025)**: These coins are a newer series and generally valued between $1 and $5.

Future of the Quarter Dollar

Thanks to the Circulating Collectible Coin Redesign Act of 2020, the Quarter Dollar will continue to serve as a canvas for innovative numismatic art. After the American Women series concludes in 2025, new coins will be minted in 2026 to celebrate the USA's 250th anniversary of independence. From 2027 to 2030, the U.S. Mint will issue five new quarter dollars per year, each highlighting a sport played by American youth, with each coin featuring a new likeness of George Washington on the obverse.

→ QUARTERMAN'S SELECTION OF COINS

1917 Standing Liberty Quarter: Type 1

It was produced in 1916 with a very low mintage. Thus, the 1916 Standing Liberty quarter is very uncommon and costly.

Subsequently, the second production year in 1917 is considerably fair in a standard U.S. coin price sample.

The Type 1-coin characteristics of Lady Liberty leave her left breast uncovered. Some people think that the outrage flashed by the people resulted in the production of the second coin type by the U.S. Mint covering Lady Liberty's chest with a coat of chain mail. A different theory is that the U.S. was getting ready for arrival into World War I in 1917, and the coat of chain mail was included to specify that Lady Liberty was prepared for battle. Distributed coin examples are low-priced for even a starter collector. A middle coin collector can effortlessly get uncirculated samples.

The 2004 Wisconsin State Quarter with Extra Leaf

If you are a State Quarter fanatic, this coin may be a very interesting one to collect. 453 million of this Quarter were minted in 2004. Of these, several thousand somehow ended up with an extra leaf on a husk of corn on the tail's side. It is said that a mint employee intentionally made this 'mistake.' The error is what makes this coin valuable to collectors. The quality of the coin considered; the 'extra leaf' quarters fetch up to $1499. About five thousand of the Quarters have been found in Tucson. Therefore, if you live around this area, you may want to double-check your pocket change or your coin jar. You don't know, you might be one of the lucky owners of the Extra Leaf State Quarter.

1/4 Dollar (Washington) 1965-1998S of the United States

Features:

Name: 1/4 dollar (Washington)

Shape: Round

Material: Copper-nickel

Weight (g): 5,67 g

Diameter (mm): 24,30 mm

Edge: Fluted

Price: 0,10$ - 750,00$.

The 25-cent coin (cora, quarter, or quarter dollar) is a denomination currently in circulation in the United States since 1796.

The reverse of the coins minted until 1998 has as design a bald eagle, (not related to the obverse design of the Great Seal of the

United States), the name of the country, the traditional motto (E Pluribus Unum), and the face value.

The obverse features the word contained on all Liberty U.S. Dollar coins, the official motto (In God We Trust), a portrait of the first U.S. President George Washington, and the year in which the coin was produced.

1/4 Dollar (50 States of the USA - Georgia) 1999D-1999S of the United States of America

The 1/4-dollar (50 States of the USA - Georgia) coin of 1999D-1999S belongs to the United States coin catalog.

Features:

Name: 1/4 dollar (50 States of the USA - Georgia)

Shape: Round

Material: Copper-nickel

Weight (g): 5,67 g

Diameter (mm): 24,26 mm

1/4 Dollar (50 U.S. States - Connecticut) 1999D-1999S of the United States

The 1/4-dollar (50 States of the USA - Connecticut) coin of 1999D-1999S belongs to the United States coin catalog.

Features:

Name: 1/4 dollar (50 States of the USA - Connecticut)

Shape: Round

Material: Copper alloy with cupro-nickel plating

1/4 Dollar (Washington Quarter, Bicentennial) 1976 of the United States of America

The 1/4-dollar (Washington Quarter, Bicentennial) coin of 1976 belongs to the United States coin catalog.

Features:

Name:/4 dollar (Washington Quarter, Bicentennial)

Shape: Round

Material: Silver (0,400)

Weight (g):5,75 g

Diameter (mm):24,26 mm

Edge: Fluted

Price: 40,00$ - 450,00$.

The Jefferson 1/4 Dollar (Famous Women - Anna May Wong) 2022D-2022S of the United States

The 1/4-dollar (Famous Women - Anna May Wong) coin of 2022D-2022S belongs to the United States coin catalog. You can find this coin in users' collections and find out its numismatic value.

How Much Are the 1/4 Dollar Coins (Famous Women - Anna May Wong) Worth? The price ranges from 1,00€ to 1,30€ depending on the mint condition. You can see all the prices of this coin in the description; the values are calculated with the market price that people assign to their collections according to its state of conservation and other criteria.

Features:

Name: 1/4 dollar (Famous women - Anna May Wong).

Shape: Round

Material: Copper-plated copper-nickel plated

Weight (g): 5,67 g

Diameter (mm): 24,30 mm

Edge: Plain - Obverse: LIBERTY IN GOD WE TRUST 2022 P

Reverse: - UNITED STATES OF AMERICA - QUARTER DOLLAR - ANNA MAY WONG - E PLURIBUS UNUM

Price: 1,00$ - 1,30$.

DIME

The U.S. dime, a small but significant coin, has been minted since 1796. Here's a detailed guide to its major versions and their values.

Draped Bust (1796-1807)

The **Draped Bust Dime (1796-1807)** features two main versions:

- **Small Eagle Reverse (1796-1797)**: These coins are rare and highly sought after, with values ranging from $2,000 to over $20,000 depending on condition.
- **Heraldic Eagle Reverse (1798-1807)**: Featuring a stronger eagle design, these coins generally range from $1,000 to $15,000.

Capped Bust (1809-1837)

The **Capped Bust Dime (1809-1837)** comes in two varieties:

- **Variety 1 - Wide Border (1809-1828)**: These coins typically range from $100 to $1,500.
- **Variety 2 - Modified Design (1828-1837)**: Values for these coins range from $50 to $1,000.

Liberty Seated (1837-1891)

The **Liberty Seated Dime (1837-1891)** has several varieties:

- **Variety 1 - No Stars on Obverse (1837-1838)**: Values range from $50 to $500.
- **Variety 2 - Stars on Obverse (1838-1853)**: Typically valued between $20 and $300.
- **Variety 3 - Arrows at Date (1853-1855)**: Ranges from $25 to $250.
- **Variety 4 - Legend on Obverse (1860-1873)**: Values generally range from $15 to $200.
- **Variety 5 - Arrows at Date (1873-1874)**: These coins typically range from $20 to $300.

Barber (1892-1916)

The **Barber Dime (1892-1916)**, known for its classical design, generally ranges in value from $5 to $500, with higher prices for better conditions and rare dates.

Mercury Dime (1916-1945)

The **Mercury Dime (1916-1945)** is a favorite among collectors for its beautiful design. Values range from $2 to $50 for common dates in average condition, with rare dates and high grades fetching significantly more.

Roosevelt (1946 to Date)

The **Roosevelt Dime (1946 to date)** includes two main versions:

- **Silver Coinage (1946-1964)**: Typically valued between $2 and $15.
- **Clad Coinage and Silver Proofs (1965 to date)**: Generally range from face value to $5, with some proofs and special issues worth more.

→ **QUARTERMAN'S SELECTION OF COINS**

The 1982 No-Mint Mark Roosevelt Dime

In 1982, the Philadelphia mint erroneously omitted the letter 'p' on the Roosevelt Dime. This means that this coin does not have a mint mark. It is not clear how many of these were distributed but up to 10,000 have been recorded to be in existence. It has a face value of $0. 10 but in the numismatic world, it is estimated to have a value of $300.

It has no mint mark and a face value of $0.01, but no mint mark. It is estimated to be worth $300. All U.S. coins bear a letter denoting the mint where they were struck, with the letters corresponding to the names of cities.

The Philadelphia Mint accidentally omitted the letter "P" from the Roosevelt dime in 1982. No one knows the exact number of these distributed coins, but as many as 10,000 have been identified. If you discover a Roosevelt dime without a mint mark, you can get close to $300 for it.

1 Dime (Seated Liberty) 1840-1850 from the United States

The 1 dime (Seated Liberty) coin of 1840-1850 belongs to the United States coin catalog.

Features:

Name: 1 dime (Seated Liberty)

Shape: Round

Material: Silver

Weight (g): 2,70 g

Diameter (mm): 17,90 mm

Price: It can be worth $25 in average conditions and between $380 and $738 or more without circulation.

1 Dime (10 cents) (Roosevelt Silver Dime) 1946-1964D

The 1 dime (10 cents) (Roosevelt Silver Dime) coin of 1946-1964D belongs to the United States coin catalog.

Features:

Name: 1 dime (10 cents) (Roosevelt Silver Dime)

Shape: Round

Material: Silver (0,900)

Weight (g): 2.50 g

Diameter (mm): 17,90 mm

Edge: Fluted

Price: 1,00$ - 650,00$.

1 Dime (10 cents) (Roosevelt Dime) 1965-2022P

The 1 dime (10 cents) (Roosevelt Dime) coin of 1965-2022P belongs to the United States coin catalog.

Features:

Name: 1 dime (10 cents) (Roosevelt Dime)

Shape: Round

Material: Copper-nickel

Weight (g):2,27 g

Diameter (mm):17,90 mm

Edge: Fluted

Price: 0,05$ - 742,00$.

The U.S. Half Dime, a precursor to the modern nickel, was minted from 1794 to 1873. Here's a comprehensive guide to its main versions and their values.

Flowing Hair (1794-1795)

The **Flowing Hair Half Dime (1794-1795)** is the earliest half dime issued by the U.S. Mint. Featuring Liberty with flowing hair on the obverse and a small eagle on the reverse, these coins are rare and highly prized. Values typically range from $1,000 to over $20,000, depending on condition.

Draped Bust (1796-1805)

The **Draped Bust Half Dime (1796-1805)** comes in two main versions:

- **Small Eagle Reverse (1796-1797)**: Known for its delicate eagle design, these coins are valued between $1,500 and $25,000.
- **Heraldic Eagle Reverse (1800-1805)**: Featuring a stronger eagle design, these coins generally range from $1,000 to $10,000.

Capped Bust (1829-1837)

The **Capped Bust Half Dime (1829-1837)** is noted for its intricate design. These coins are typically valued between $30 and $1,000, depending on the year and condition.

Liberty Seated (1837-1873)

The **Liberty Seated Half Dime (1837-1873)** has several varieties:

- **Variety 1 - No Stars on Obverse (1837-1839)**: These early versions are valued between $30 and $500.
- **Variety 2 - Stars on Obverse (1838-1853)**: Typically valued between $20 and $300.
- **Variety 3 - Arrows at Date (1853-1855)**: Values range from $25 to $250.
- **Variety 4 - Legend on Obverse (1860-1873)**: These coins generally range from $15 to $200.

→ **QUARTERMAN'S SELECTION OF COINS**

1 Half Dime (Seated Liberty) 1870-1872 of the United States

The 1 half dime (Seated Liberty) from 1870-1872 belongs to the United States coin catalog.

Features:

Name: 1 half dime (Seated Liberty)

Shape: Round

Material: Silver

Weight: 12,5 g

Diameter: 15,5 mm

1/2 Dime (Seated Liberty) 1853 of the United States of America

The 1/2 dime (Seated Liberty) of 1853 belongs to the United States coin catalog.

Features:

Name: 1/2 dime (Seated Liberty)

Shape: Round

Material: Silver (0,900)

Weight (g): 1,24 g

Diameter (mm): 15,50 mm

1/2 Dime (Seated Liberty) 1853 of the United States of America United States 1 Dime (Seated Liberty Dime) 1853-1855

The 1 dime (Seated Liberty Dime) from 1853-1855 belongs to the United States coin catalog.

Features:

Name: 1 dime (Seated Liberty Dime)

Shape: Round

Material: Silver

Weight (g): 2,70 g

Diameter (mm): 17,90 mm

NICKEL FIVE-CENT PIECES

The U.S. Nickel, first minted in 1866, is a staple of American coinage. Here's a comprehensive guide to its main versions and their values.

Shield (1866-1883)

The **Shield Nickel (1866-1883)** is the first five-cent piece made of nickel. It features a shield on the obverse and a wreath on the reverse. These coins are generally valued between $20 and $200, depending on their condition and specific year, with some rare varieties fetching higher prices.

Liberty Head (1883-1913)

The **Liberty Head Nickel (1883-1913)**, also known as the "V" Nickel due to the

Roman numeral on the reverse, features Liberty on the obverse. Early issues (1883) lacked the word "CENTS" and are worth $10 to $100. Later issues with "CENTS" (1883-1913) range from $5 to $200, with the extremely rare 1913 issue being one of the most valuable U.S. coins, worth millions.

Indian Head or Buffalo (1913-1938)

The **Indian Head or Buffalo Nickel (1913-1938)** is a beloved design among collectors. It has two varieties:

- **Variety 1 - Five Cents on Raised Ground (1913)**: These coins are valued between $20 and $150.
- **Variety 2 - Five Cents in Recess (1913-1938)**: More common, they typically range from $10 to $50, with higher prices for rare dates and mint marks.

Jefferson (1938-2003)

The **Jefferson Nickel (1938-2003)** has seen several variations:

- **Wartime Silver Alloy (1942-1945)**: Due to nickel shortages during WWII, these nickels contain silver and are valued between $1 and $10.
- **Prewar Composition, Mintmark Style Resumed (1946-1965)**: These coins range from face value to a few dollars for well-preserved examples.

Westward Journey (2004-2005)

The **Westward Journey Nickels (2004-2005)** commemorate the Lewis and Clark expedition with different reverse designs. These modern coins are generally valued at face value, though special proofs and mint errors can be worth more.

Jefferson Modified (2006 to Date)

The **Jefferson Nickel (2006 to date)** features a modified design with a forward-facing portrait of Jefferson. These are mostly valued at face value, though certain proof and special issue coins can have higher values.

→ QUARTERMAN'S SELECTION OF COINS

The 2005 Speared Bison Jefferson Nickel

On the back of this Nickel is a buffalo that appears to be pierced from underneath. This is an error that occurred when the die got a scratch at the time of minting the coin. It makes a beautiful detail on the coin. However, this coin is not considered to be very valuable; it has a face value of $0.5 but there was an exception. It is reported that a 2005-D 5C Speared Bison Jefferson Nickel was sold for up to $ 1,265 at an auction.

5 Cents (Liberty Nickel) 1883-1912S of the United States

The 5 cents (Liberty Nickel) coin of 1883-1912S belongs to the United States coin catalog. You can find this coin in users' collections and find out its numismatic value.

Jefferson 5-cent Nickel

Features:

Name: 5 cents (Liberty Nickel).

Shape: Round

Material: Copper-nickel

Weight (g):5,00 g

Diameter (mm):21.20 mm

Edge: Plain; Price: 1,25$ - 650,00$.

The Jefferson nickel has been the nickel coin of the United States since 1938 when it entered circulation to replace the Buffalo Nickel. It features the face of former U.S. President Thomas Jefferson on one side and his home, Monticello, on the other.

The nickel or Jefferson nickel (colloquially called "nickel") is a circulating coin in the United States. There are several versions of this coin; the current one is called "Jefferson nickel," although the first one was called "half dime" and was minted during the 1790s.

Features:

Diameter: 21.21 mm

Thickness: 1.95 mm.

Weight: 5.00 grams

Alloy: 75% copper + 25% nickel

Edge: smooth

Note: The ten rarest and most valuable nickels have already been sold, but some are still in the hands of U.S. citizens. Jefferson nickels can be worth thousands of dollars.

1966 Nickell

The second most important date on these coins is 1966, and they are priced at around $7800. "It is an extreme rarity with full steps; PCGS has certified only six examples," said the same agency.

Features:

Mint: Philadelphia "P"

Composition: 75% Copper + 25% Nickel

Weight: 5 grams

Diameter: 21.2 mm

Series: Jefferson Nickel Cents (1946-2003)

Preservation Grade: EF-45

Certification: uncertified

5 Cents (Jefferson) 1946-2003S of the United States

The 5 cents (Jefferson) coin of 1946-2003S belongs to the United States coin catalog.

Features:

Name: 5 cents (Jefferson)

Shape: Round

Material: Copper-nickel

Weight (g): 5.00 g

Diameter (mm): 21.21 mm

Edge: Smooth

Price: 0,04$ - 750,00$.

CENTS

The **One Cent** coin has evolved significantly since its inception:

- **Flowing Hair (1793):**
  - **Chain Reverse (1793):** Rare and valuable, typically between $2,000 and $20,000.
  - **Wreath Reverse (1793):** Generally valued from $1,000 to $10,000.
- **Liberty Cap (1793-1796):** Values range from $500 to $5,000.
- **Draped Bust (1796-1807):** Typically valued between $200 and $2,500.

- **Classic Head (1808-1814):** These coins range from $100 to $1,500.
- **Liberty Head or Matron Head (1816-1857):** Values range from $20 to $800.
- **Flying Eagle (1856-1858):** Highly collectible, with values ranging from $30 to $2,000.
- **Indian Head (1859-1909):**
  - **Variety 1 - Copper Nickel, Laurel Wreath Reverse (1859):** Typically valued from $20 to $300.
  - **Variety 2 - Copper Nickel, Oak Wreath with Shield (1860-1864):** Values range from $15 to $200.
  - **Variety 3 - Bronze (1864-1909):** Generally valued between $1 and $50.

Lincoln Cent

The **Lincoln Cent** is one of the most recognized U.S. coins:

- **Wheat Ears Reverse (1909-1958):**
  - **Variety 1 - Bronze (1909-1942):** Values range from $1 to $10,000, with key dates fetching higher prices.

- **Variety 2 - Zinc-Coated Steel (1943)**: Typically valued between $0.10 and $1.00.
- **Variety 1 Resumed (Bronze - 1944-1958)**: Values range from $0.10 to $5.00.
- **Lincoln, Memorial Reverse (1959-2008)**:
  - **Copper Alloy (1959-1982)**: Generally valued at face value to $0.50.
  - **Copper-Plated Zinc (1982-2008)**: Typically face value to $0.10.
- **Lincoln, Bicentennial (2009)**: Valued at face value to $0.50.
- **Lincoln, Shield Reverse (2010 to date)**: Generally face value to $0.10.

Silver Three-Cent Pieces

The **Silver Three-Cent Piece**, minted from 1851 to 1873, is an unusual denomination with unique appeal:

- Values typically range from $20 to $500, with higher prices for coins in excellent condition or rare dates.

→ QUARTERMAN'S SELECTION OF COINS

1 Cent (Liberty Head / Matron Head) 1831 of United States of America

The 1-cent (Liberty Head / Matron Head) coin of 1831 belongs to the United States coin catalog.

Features:

Name: 1 cent (Liberty Head / Matron Head)

Shape: Round

Material: Copper

Weight (g): 10,85 g

Diameter (mm): 28,50 mm

Edge: Plain

Price: $290.00

1 Cent 1828 of the United States

The 1 cent 1828 coin belongs to the United States coin catalog.

Features:

Name: 1 cent

Shape: Round

Material: Copper

Weight (g): 10.89 g

Diameter (mm): 28,00 mm

Price: It can be worth $46 in average condition and between $1,421 and $3,154 or more in new uncirculated condition.

1 Cent (Braided Hair cent) 1840-1845 of the United States of America

The 1 cent (Braided Hair cent) coin of 1840-1845 belongs to the United States coin catalog.

Features:

Name: 1 cent (Braided Hair cent)

Shape: Round

Material: Copper

Weight (g): 10,89 g

Diameter (mm): 27,50 mm

Price: $28,92

United States 3 Cents (type 1) 1851-1853

The 3 cents (type 1) coin of 1851-1853 belongs to the United States coin catalog.

Features:

Name: 3 cents (type 1)

Shape: Round

Material: Silver (0,750)

Weight (g): 0,80 g

Diameter (mm): 14,00 mm

1 Cent (Flying Eagle cent) 1856-1858 of the United States of America

The 1-cent (Flying Eagle cent) coin of 1856-1858 belongs to the United States coin catalog.

Features:

Name: 1 cent (Flying Eagle cent)

Shape: Round

Material: Copper-nickel

Weight (g): 4,87 g

Diameter (mm): 19,00 mm

United States 1 Cent (Indian Head cent) 1859

The 1-cent (Indian Head cent) coin of 1859 belongs to the United States coin catalog.

Features:

Name: 1 cent (Indian Head cent)

Shape: Round

Material: Copper-nickel

Weight (g): 4,67 g

Diameter (mm): 19,00 mm

1 Cent (Indian Head cent) 1860-1864 of the United States of America

The 1-cent (Indian Head cent) coin of 1860-1864 belongs to the United States coin catalog.

Features:

Name: 1 cent (Indian Head cent)

Shape: Round

Material: Copper-nickel

Weight (g): 4,67 g

Diameter (mm): 19,00 mm

1 Cent (Indian Head cent) 1864-1909S of the United States

The 1 cent (Indian Head cent) coin of 1864-1909S is from the United States coin catalog.

Features:

Name: 1 cent (Indian Head cent)

Shape: Round

Material: Bronze

Weight (g): 3,11 g

Diameter (mm): 19,00 mm

1 Cent (Lincoln Memorial) 1959-1982 United States Coin

The 1-cent (Lincoln Memorial) coin of 1959-1982S belongs to the United States coin catalog.

Features:

Name: 1 cent (Lincoln Memorial)

Shape: Round - Material: Brass

Weight (g): 3.11 g - Diameter (mm): 19.00 mm

Edge: Smooth

Price: 0,01$ - 800,00 $.

3 Cents (type 2) 1854-1858 of the United States

The 3 cents (type 2) coin of 1854-1858 belongs to the United States coin catalog.

Features:

Name: 3 cents (type 2)

Shape: Round

Material: Silver

Weight (g): 0,75 g

Diameter (mm): 14,00 mm

3 Cents 1859-1873 United States Coin

The 3-cents 1859-1873 coin belongs to the United States coin catalog.

Features:

Name: 3 cents

Shape: Round

Material: Silver (0,750)

Weight (g): 0,75 g

Diameter (mm): 14,00 mm

Lincoln Cents

The Lincoln cent is one of the most versatile coins in American history. In 1909, the first Lincoln cent was struck. The initial versions of the coin depicted two wheat stalks.

Since the first editions, numerous upgrades and revisions have been made to the coins, and today there are hundreds of variants. Fortunately, some of these versions are now in circulation, so I recommend beginning with those. Because they are considered "common" coins, their value is typically not particularly high, but you can easily find different editions on eBay and other online marketplaces.

1909-S V.D.B. Lincoln Cent

In 1909, the United States altered the one-cent coin design from the India Head to a design commemorating the 100th anniversary of President Abraham Lincoln's birth. The coin was immediately successful to the public. Alternatively, Victor David Brenner put his three abbreviations on the converse of the penny close to the bottom. Former designers use just their last abbreviation, and a mint designer known as Charles Barber changed the new trend. Before the United States Mint facility was established in San Francisco, 484,000 new Lincoln pennies were made and the abbreviations at the back were taken away. This modification in the design resulted in an immediate scarcity.

Although, some may claim that the 1909-S VDB Lincoln Cent is the commonest amongst the U.S. coin. Many coin collectors started the journey of their coin-collecting when they picked Lincoln pennies. The 1909-S VDB is the "Holy Grail" of Lincoln pennies with its insufficiency. This uncommon coin is always the last coin of Lincoln currency collectors that will add up to their coin collecting. For some time now, this coin has preserved its significance and reputation amongst collectors of U.S. coins.

1914-D Lincoln Cent

Even though it's not as uncommon as the 1909-S V.D.B. Lincoln cent, the 1914-D coin comes in a nearby close to a mintage of 1,193,000 coins made. What necessitates the requirement of this coin is that undistributed specimens were not stored in the similar amounts that the 1909-S V.D.B. coins also were. Hence, uncirculated 1914-D patterns are more uncommon than the more prevalent 1909-S V.D.B. coins.

Due to the popular nature of the Lincoln cents and the coin collectors, the coin has sustained its value over time, especially for middle and skillful collectors looking for a quality-undistributed coin. Nevertheless, distributed specimens are also within the coin-collecting budget of starting and middle coin collectors. Be watchful while looking for a distributed specimen, sort for a properly toned coin with no difficulties like dings or scratches.

The 1943 Lincoln Head Copper Penny

This is a copper coin that was minted during a time when copper was desperately needed for the war effort and was not being used to make coins. The copper penny collection happened by chance. During this period, the most common pennies were made of silver and coated with silver to give them a gleaming appearance. During this time, very few copper coins were produced. This is why the 1943 Lincoln Head Copper Penny is so valuable and can fetch up to $10,000.

While copper and nickel were traditionally used to make pennies, the United States needed the metals for its war effort, so the mint began using steel instead. However, a mistaken batch of copper pennies was still struck, possibly due to blanks still in the process when the mint began producing modern steel pennies. Though some claim there are only 20 of these pennies left, experts believe there could be up to forty of them.

According to the United States Mint, such coins are frequently counterfeited because it is relatively easy to cover steel pennies in copper and change the date on 1945, 1948, and 1949 coins. However, if the coin clings to a magnet, you can tell if it is made of steel.

While an ordinary steel 1943 Lincoln penny could fetch 30 to 45 cents — roughly 30 or 40 times its face value — the unique copper ones fetched $204,000 in a 2019 market. The young man who discovered this example of the currency in his school canteens kept it for nearly 70 years.

According to Coin Week, a variation of this coin sold at auction for $1.75 million in 2010.

The coin is worth $0.01, and the mint mark is an S. It is thought to be worth $10,000. Copper pennies are now commonplace, but this was not always the case.

Copper was required for the war effort in 1943, so it was not used to create coins then. Despite this, a copper batch was produced by accident. Since very few copper pennies left factories during this period, those that did could be worth up to $10,000.

The 1969-S Lincoln Cent with Double Die Obverse

This is a very special coin. It was the only one to be featured On America's 'most wanted' list of the Federal Bureau of Investigation. Beware that there may be fake ones still circulating as this was one coin that counterfeiters Morton Goodman and Roy Gray produced very similar coins to these, thus attracting overwhelming attention from the authorities. It is reported that less than a hundred authentic pieces were produced. Because of its rarity, it attracts high prices. Actually, it has an estimated value of up to $126,000 in auctions.

1955 Doubled-Die Obverse Lincoln Cent

The 1955 Doubled-Die Lincoln cent is a unique coin that is highly sought after by Lincoln penny collectors. Despite the fact that this is a mistake coin, many collectors want to add one to their collection. The coin is without a doubt the most well-known error coin produced by the United States Mint.

The story of this error coin began when the United States Mint used a coin die and received double brands with a slight counterbalance from each of them. After approximately 20,000 to 24,000 coins were freely mixed and available with a batch of correctly produced coins, mint workers discovered the error. The mint later realized that the expense of melting the entire amount of coins to scrap the false coins that had become mixed in was not worth it.

When the update to this error coin began to appear in local papers in the northeastern United States, many people removed the coins from circulation. Local coin shops were buying them as fast as they could be obtained. There are numerous undistributed and near uncirculated examples available for your various collections.

Regrettably, this is one of the most counterfeit coins on the market. Many of these excellent forgeries originated in China. Be wary of any coins purchased on eBay or from any seller you do not know. Building a relationship with a trustworthy dealer is a good way to invest in coins.

Unlocking the Rich History of Coinage: Your Guide to Starting a Valuable Collection of UK, Canadian, and Australian Coins

The history of coinage in the United Kingdom, Canada, and Australia is a captivating journey that mirrors each nation's development and cultural heritage. From the establishment of the Royal Mint in London to the mints in Ottawa and Canberra, the progression of coinage in these countries has been marked by significant milestones and changes. Each era introduced unique designs and minting technologies, reflecting the evolving identities and economies of these nations.

Regular mint issues from the UK, Canada, and Australia encompass a wide range of denominations and designs, each with its own distinctive features and historical importance. Understanding the role of different mints and their corresponding mint marks is crucial for any collector. These marks not only indicate the coin's origin but also enhance its rarity and value, particularly in cases of limited mintages.

Here is a list of notable coins from the UK, Canada, and Australia to help you start building your collection. All of them are excellent choices for both novice and seasoned collectors.

United Kingdom Coins

1. **Gold Sovereign (1817-Present)**

   - **Origin**: Introduced during the reign of King George III.

   - **Characteristics**: Features a depiction of St. George slaying the dragon on the reverse and the reigning monarch's portrait on the obverse.

   - **Current Value**: Typically valued between $400 and $600, depending on the condition and year.

2. **1902 Edward VII Crown**

- **Origin**: Issued during the coronation of Edward VII.
- **Characteristics**: Silver coin featuring a crowned Edward VII on the obverse and a depiction of St. George and the dragon on the reverse.
- **Current Value**: Generally ranges from $200 to $1,000 based on condition.

3. **1937 George VI Coronation Crown**

- **Origin**: Issued to commemorate the coronation of King George VI.
- **Characteristics**: Features the crowned bust of George VI on the obverse and a depiction of St. George and the dragon on the reverse.
- **Current Value**: Valued between $100 and $300.

4. **1977 Silver Jubilee Crown**

- **Origin**: Issued to mark the Silver Jubilee of Queen Elizabeth II.
- **Characteristics**: Features a portrait of Queen Elizabeth II on the obverse and a royal coat of arms on the reverse.
- **Current Value**: Typically valued between $20 and $50.

5. **1847 Gothic Crown**

- **Origin**: Known for its intricate gothic design.
- **Characteristics**: Features a detailed portrait of Queen Victoria on the obverse.
- **Current Value**: Ranges from $500 to $5,000.

6. **1819 George III Half Crown**

- **Origin**: Issued during the reign of King George III.
- **Characteristics**: Features a profile of George III on the obverse.
- **Current Value**: Typically valued between $200 and $1,200.

7. **1887 Queen Victoria Double Florin**

- **Origin**: Issued during the Golden Jubilee of Queen Victoria.

- **Characteristics**: Features the Jubilee portrait of Queen Victoria on the obverse.

- **Current Value**: Ranges from $50 to $300.

8. **1696 William III Crown**

- **Origin**: Issued during the reign of William III.

- **Characteristics**: Features a portrait of William III on the obverse.

- **Current Value**: Generally valued between $500 and $3,000.

9. **1816 George III Sixpence**

- **Origin**: Issued during the reign of George III.

- **Characteristics**: Features a profile of George III on the obverse.

- **Current Value**: Valued between $50 and $400.

10. **2002 Golden Jubilee Crown**

- **Origin**: Issued to celebrate the Golden Jubilee of Queen Elizabeth II.

- **Characteristics**: Features a double portrait of the Queen on the obverse.

- **Current Value**: Typically valued between $10 and $50.

Canadian Coins

1. **1921 50 Cent Piece**

- **Origin**: Known as the "King of Canadian Coins" due to its rarity.

- **Characteristics**: Features the portrait of King George V on the obverse and a coat of arms on the reverse.

- **Current Value**: Valued at over $50,000 depending on condition.

2. **1936 Dot Cent**

- **Origin**: An unusual coin with a small dot below the date, minted during a transitional period.

- **Characteristics**: Features King George V on the obverse.

- **Current Value**: Typically ranges from $5,000 to $10,000.

3. **1948 Silver Dollar**

   - **Origin**: Known for its low mintage and historical significance.

   - **Characteristics**: Features a portrait of King George VI on the obverse and a canoe with indigenous people on the reverse.

   - **Current Value**: Valued between $1,000 and $3,000.

4. **1911 Silver Dollar**

   - **Origin**: Extremely rare, with only a few specimens known.

   - **Characteristics**: Features King George V on the obverse.

   - **Current Value**: Can exceed $500,000.

5. **1935 Voyageur Dollar**

   - **Origin**: The first silver dollar issued by Canada.

   - **Characteristics**: Features a voyageur and indigenous guide in a canoe.

   - **Current Value**: Ranges from $100 to $1,000.

6. **1925 5 Cent Coin**

   - **Origin**: Known for its rarity.

   - **Characteristics**: Features King George V on the obverse.

   - **Current Value**: Typically ranges from $500 to $2,000.

7. **1967 Centennial Coins**

   - **Origin**: Issued to celebrate Canada's centennial.

   - **Characteristics**: Features various Canadian wildlife.

   - **Current Value**: Generally valued between $10 and $100, depending on the denomination.

8. **1987 Loon Dollar ("Loonie")**

- **Origin**: Canada's first $1 coin featuring a loon.

- **Characteristics**: Features a loon on the reverse.

- **Current Value**: Generally face value to $10, special editions can be more.

Australian Coins

1. **1930 Penny**

   - **Origin**: One of Australia's most famous rare coins.

   - **Characteristics**: Features King George V on the obverse.

   - **Current Value**: Can fetch up to $30,000 depending on condition.

2. **1910 Florin**

   - **Origin**: Australia's first florin, minted during the reign of King Edward VII.

   - **Characteristics**: Features a crowned and draped bust of Edward VII on the obverse.

   - **Current Value**: Typically valued between $200 and $1,000.

→ QUARTERMAN'S SELECTION OF COINS

(1) George III Sovereign (1817):

Obverse: Bust of King George III with the inscription "GEORGIUS III D.G. BRITANNIAR: REX F.D."

Reverse: Saint George slaying the dragon, designed by Benedetto Pistrucci, with the year of issue.

Features:

Diameter: 22.05 mm

Thickness: 1.52 mm

Weight: 7.98 grams

Alloy: 22-carat gold (91.67% gold, 8.33% copper)

Edge: Milled

Grade	Description	Market Value (GBP)
F	Good definition of the main details	£600-700
VF	Slight wear on high points, detailed portrait.	£900-1000
EF	Minor marks only, crisp details	£2000-2200
UNC	Full mint lustre, no wear	£4500-5000
Mintage	Varies significantly, with earlier years having lower mintages	3.235.239

(2) Victoria Sovereign (1841)

Obverse: Features the young Queen Victoria's effigy. Inscription: "VICTORIA DEI GRATIA". Year of issue inscribed.

Reverse: Crowned shield of arms within a wreath. Inscription: "VICTORIA D.G. BRITANNIARUM REGINA F.D."

Features:

Diameter: 22.05 mm

Thickness: 1.52 mm

Weight: 7.98 grams

Alloy: 22-carat gold (91.67% gold, 8.33% copper)

Edge: Milled

Grade	Description	Market Value (GBP)
F	Good definition of the main details	£5.000
VF	Slight wear on high points, detailed portrait.	£10.000
EF	Minor marks only, crisp details	£20.000
UNC	Full mint lustre, no wear	–
Mintage	Varies significantly, with earlier years having lower mintages	124,054

(3) Victoria Half Sovereign (1872)

Obverse: Features the young Queen Victoria's portrait. Inscription:

"VICTORIA DEI GRATIA." Year of issue inscribed.

Reverse: Crowned shield of arms. Inscription: "VICTORIA D.G. BRITANNIARUM: REGINA F.D."

Features:

Diameter: 19.30 mm

Thickness: 1.02 mm

Weight: 3.99 grams

Alloy: 22-carat gold (91.67% gold, 8.33% copper)

Edge: Milled

Grade	Description	Market Value (GBP)
F	Good definition of the main details	£150-200
VF	Slight wear on high points, detailed portrait.	£200-250
EF	Minor marks only, crisp details	£650-700
UNC	Full mint lustre, no wear	£1000-1100
Mintage	Varies significantly, with earlier years	3.248.627

	having lower mintages	

(4) Edward VII Half Sovereign (1902)

Obverse: Bust of King Edward VII with the inscription "EDWARDVS VII D.G. BRITT OMN REX F.D. IND IMP"

Reverse: Saint George slaying the dragon with the year of issue.

BRITANNIARUM: REGINA F.D."

Features:

Diameter: 19.30 mm

Thickness: 1.02 mm

Weight: 3.99 grams

Alloy: 22-carat gold (91.67% gold, 8.33% copper)

Edge: Milled

Grade	Description	Market Value (GBP)
F	Good definition of the main details	£150-200
VF	Slight wear on high points, detailed portrait.	£200-250

EF	Minor marks only, crisp details	£250-300
UNC	Full mint lustre, no wear	£450-500
Mintage	Varies significantly, with earlier years having lower mintages	4.244.457

(5) Victoria Gothic Head Issues (1847)

Obverse: Queen Victoria in Gothic style with the inscription "VICTORIA DEI GRATIA BRITANNIAR: REG F.D."

Reverse: Four shields of arms surrounded by the Order of the Garter.

Features:

Diameter: 38.61 mm

Thickness: 3.0 mm

Weight: 28.28 grams

Alloy: .925 silver

Edge: Milled

Grade	Description	Market Value (GBP)
F	Good definition of the main details	£1200
VF	Slight wear on high points, detailed portrait.	£2500
EF	Minor marks only, crisp details	£4500
UNC	Full mint lustre, no wear	£12000
Mintage	Varies significantly, with earlier years having lower mintages	8.000

(6) George V Silver Crown (1935)

Jubilee issue. Incuse edge inscription

Obverse: George V's profile.

Reverse: Saint George slaying the dragon, commonly known as the "Rocking Horse" design.

Features:

Diameter: 38.61 mm

Thickness: 3.0 mm

Weight: 28.28 grams

Alloy: .925 silver

Edge: Milled

Grade	Description	Market Value (GBP)
F	Good definition of the main details	£15
VF	Slight wear on high points, detailed portrait.	£25
EF	Minor marks only, crisp details	£30
UNC	Full mint lustre, no wear	£50
Mintage	Varies significantly, with earlier years having lower mintages	714.769

Note: Error edge inscription £ 1500 | Gold Proof extremely rare

(7) Edward VII Half Crown (1910)

Obverse: Portrait of King Edward VII facing right. Inscription: "EDWARDVS VII D.G. BRITT: OMN: REX F.D. IND: IMP:"

Reverse Features a crowned shield with the coat of arms of the United Kingdom, flanked by the emblems of England, Scotland, and Ireland. Inscription: "FID DEF IND IMP HALF CROWN 1909"

Features:

Diameter: 32.31 mm

Thickness: 2.3 mm

Weight: 14.14 grams

Alloy: .925 silver (92.5% silver, 7.5% copper)

Edge: Milled

Grade	Description	Market Value (GBP)
F	Good definition of the main details	£15
VF	Slight wear on high points, detailed portrait.	£60
EF	Minor marks only, crisp details	£350

UNC	Full mint lustre, no wear	£900
Mintage	Varies significantly, with earlier years having lower mintages	3.051.592

(8) Elizabeth II Half Crown (1959)

Obverse: Portrait of Queen Elizabeth II facing right.

Inscription: "ELIZABETH II DEI GRATIA REGINA F:D:"

Reverse: Features a crowned shield with the coat of arms of the United Kingdom, flanked by the symbols of England, Scotland, and Ireland.

Inscription: "FID DEF HALF CROWN 1959"

Features:

Diameter: 32.31 mm

Thickness: 2.3 mm

Weight: 14.14 grams

Alloy: Copper-nickel

Edge: Milled

Grade	Description	Market Value (GBP)
F	Good definition of the main details	-
VF	Slight wear on high points, detailed portrait.	£5
EF	Minor marks only, crisp details	£10
UNC	Full mint lustre, no wear	£40
Mintage	Varies significantly, with earlier years having lower mintages	9.028.844

(9) Victoria "Godless" Florin (1849)

Young (Crowned) Head Issues – "Godless" tpe, without D.G. "Dei Gratia".

Obverse: Young Queen Victoria facing left with the inscription "VICTORIA REGINA"

Reverse: A crowned cruciform of four shields with the emblems of England, Scotland, and Ireland, and the inscription "ONE FLORIN ONE TENTH OF A POUND"

Features:

Diameter: 28.5 mm

Thickness: 2.0 mm

Weight: 11.3 grams

Alloy: .925 silver

Edge: Milled

Grade	Description	Market Value (GBP)
F	Good definition of the main details	£30
VF	Slight wear on high points, detailed portrait.	£75
EF	Minor marks only, crisp details	£300
UNC	Full mint lustre, no wear	£600
Mintage	Varies significantly, with earlier years having lower mintages	413.820

Note: Godless Pattern only plain or milled edge (1848) extremely rare

(10) Elizabeth II Shilling E Proof-S Proof (1953)

E=England rev. (shield with three lions)

S=Scotland rev. (shield with one lion)

Obverse: Portrait of Queen Elizabeth II facing right with the inscription "ELIZABETH II DEI GRATIA REGINA"

Reverse: Features a crowned shield with three lions passant guardant representing England, with the inscription "FID DEF ONE SHILLING 1953"

Features:

Diameter: 23.6 mm

Thickness: 2.0 mm

Weight: 5.65 grams

Alloy: Copper-nickel

Edge: Milled

Grade	Description	Market Value (GBP)
F	Good definition of the main details	-
VF	Slight wear on high points, detailed portrait.	-

EF	Minor marks only, crisp details	-
UNC	Full mint lustre, no wear	£20
Mintage	Varies significantly, with earlier years having lower mintages	40.000

(11) George III Sixpence (1816) – New Coinage

Obverse: Portrait of King George III facing right, with the inscription "GEORGIUS III D:G: BRITT REX F:D:"

Reverse: Crowned shield of arms within a wreath, with the inscription "HONI SOIT PENCE"

Features:

Diameter: 19.3 mm

Thickness: 1.1 mm

Weight: 2.83 grams

Alloy: .925 silver

Edge: Milled

Grade	Description	Market Value (GBP)
F	Good definition of the main details	£7
VF	Slight wear on high points, detailed portrait.	£18
EF	Minor marks only, crisp details	£50
UNC	Full mint lustre, no wear	£150
Mintage	Varies significantly, with earlier years having lower mintages	-

⇨ Check out the cool pics of the coins described in this chapter in the bonus on the next page

☝ CLICK HERE TO DOWNLOAD IT

https://gdpublishing.aweb.page/p/5c2de7bd-8780-4c4c-afea-7444fcfe3d3a

OR SCAN QRCODE

✿ HERE IS YOU FREE GIFT!

1. **If you haven't already done so, scan the QR code** at the beginning of the book and download the Coin Identification Guide, and enjoy FREE ACCESS to Coin Hub to understand how to take coin collecting to the next level.

2. **Scan the QR code** below or simply click the link and <u>leave quick feedback on Amazon</u>!

Conclusion: The Future of Numismatics

As most of us are involved in numismatics, we do not collect for investment but as a hobby and because we enjoy it. The question is: Do you think numismatics has a future? We always want to know if our coins will be revalued, maintained, or fell into decline due to social or cultural disinterest.

Another question that many people also ask themselves is what other collections may become important in the future. It is common that, for many collectors, the impression of today's young people is not a great motivator because many are not interested in numismatics as such, but if they love collecting and are curious, it is a starting point to encourage them.

On the other hand, some think that, even if they do not do it for investment, it revalues by itself. The scarce, expensive, or most sought-after coins are increasingly difficult to find and, therefore, more expensive. The truth is that this is a road you must travel and in which you will discover and forge your theory.

What You Can Achieve Through Numismatics

I hope you find this material helpful and remember all you can accomplish through numismatics. It is not a simple collection; this term is more visualized as an auxiliary science of history that deals with the study of coins and medals. It gives valuable testimony to the peoples' exchanges and economy, as well as their political, geographical, and religious history, etc.

You should know that through numismatics, collectors get to study and discover historical facts related to wars, empires, monarchs, the evolution of art, architecture, and the traditions of nations.

Numismatics gives shape and context to the events of the past and present. Few archaeological monuments are as important as those studied by numismatics since Man has engraved his dominant ideas on them. A coin can reveal the character, customs, and historical vicissitudes that such monuments have left us.

The good thing is that, by fashion or mere investment curiosity, more and more collectors are approaching numismatics nowadays. Consequently, this hobby satisfies many and facilitates intellectual growth by acquiring new knowledge.

Its importance goes beyond the collector's mission. Since the 19th century, it is expected that the interest in learning academically about coins will continue to increase progressively until it becomes another branch of historical dissemination.

In this way, the methodology of numismatics has spread internationally and collaborates in situating and understanding the different aspects of history. It allows coin experts to know the historical periods and the role played by each society's monetary and economic spheres.

The incredible growth of the coin-collecting market has been among the most profitable in the last few years. Unfortunately, it is dangerous for the unwary, like an ocean filled with hungry sharks just looking for a chance to feast on a powerless victim.

In this book, I tried to give you the survival kit to emerge from unscathed waters and thrive.

At the same time, I showed you a method based on the 5-step. It is a fundamental process that I hope you can internalize.

I'll leave you with just this concept.

Fall in love with the process and become a master at identifying the value of a coin, recognizing the details and essential elements to value.

Most people tend to be fascinated by a single event while ignoring the process that generated that event.

That is why we get excited about setting our goals (event), but when consistently pursuing them (process), we tend to get discouraged quickly.

It is not enough to want to find a coin of value. If we don't learn to fall in love with the process, we will hardly enjoy the results of individual events.

If we want to be more constant, we must shift our focus from the final result to the daily actions contributing to that result. I have tried to show you the process that has helped me achieve my goals.

So I hope that could be the same for you and help you to achieve your investment goals.

Be careful with hungry sharks, and good luck with finding ad hidden treasures.

Made in the USA
Middletown, DE
07 September 2024